Dedicated to the Teutonic Goddess and Mrs. 42.

You are very patient wives.

TABLE OF CONTENTS

forward

Listen up, soldier. What good are you to you or anyone else if you can't decently feed yourself? Or even indecently? You need to learn three F words: Fire. Food. Fun. Two of them are even four-letters. The "Fun" is, of course, women; but the Food and Fire have to come first. First the food, because frankly we are just not sure you are manned up enough for the rest yet.

One Tuesday night back when we were both in college we were talking about women (what else?) and it came up that both of us had used our cooking skills to impress our women. We used cooking to move above the pack...cut the other studs out of the running. Alpha males with tongs. No, not tongues - although we are good with those too - tongs.

We are firm believers that every person should be able to fix a flat tire, build a fire, program a computer, construct a shed, find one of those square states out in the middle, cook a steak, fish, find everything/naughty/interesting on the internet, and learn crap you didn't already know from a book. So, we pooled our brains and money and bought the *Joy of Sex*. Oh wait, that's another story. We bought the *Joy of Cooking*. Eleven hundred and thirty-two pages of foodie delight, orgasms for the tongue, and all-around-amazing information for the kitchen. Yeah, we got a tongue theme already going on here. Think of this as "your training has already begun..."

We settled in with the bible of cooking and learned how to burn things, to create Level-7 disasters with a microwave, and to scare mortal humans out of the house. We learned to cook, to taste, to smell, to enjoy the bits and pieces of food for what they are, and how the pieces combine for a gastrointestinal orgy of delight. Our food blossomed, our sex lives improved, and people started saying silly things like "Wow, you two should open a restaurant," and "Wow, that is delicious. You two should write a book."

Years later and several million calories gone to the gut, Jim got a wild hair up his chimney and wrote down his sure-fire Hollandaise Sauce; Thomas laughed and laughed and then said, "We *should* write a cookbook." Realizing that we were surrounded by sad creatures with no food skills and lacking second dates, we realized that we had to step up and share our hard-won wisdom.

This book is that Wisdom

introduction

Do you like to eat?

No, do you REALLY like to eat?

Do you like to get lucky?

Because, my man, it is this last question that should inspire you to read on. Babes like men who cook. That's right, it gives them shudders to have you cook them a great meal. Ecstatic shudders in places you want. If you like to eat, all the more reason to read on, because frankly, you can cook stuff that tastes way better than that worthless drive-through burger you're sticking down your blow hole.

> **Tip:**
> Read all recipes through BEFORE you start. Seriously.

Are we being too harsh? Deal with it, Opie. You think bad-ass chefs like Mario Batali, Michael Symon, and Anthony Bordain got there by holding hands and singing Kumbayah? Hell no. We can tell you how to make a girl gasp with ecstasy with nothing more than a spoon. With or without food on it. So, listen up, and let's get started...

First, you're going to need to start off with something simple. If you're reading this, you probably have been mostly fed by your momma, girlfriends, or wife your entire life. Maybe they could cook like Julia Child (may she rest in peace); if so, lucky you. On the other hand, perhaps the women in your life can't tell a hand mixer from a vibrator. The days of "Home Economics" and "Miss Priss Cooking for Ladies" classes are long gone. Your female sidekick may also cook mostly with a can opener. This is unacceptable. Let's show the world how real men do it.

The Stove

Let's start with the stove; in other words, fire. You get fire, right? You can turn that little burner knob, get your Fight Guild on, and torch something. We understand. Let's not do that, but we appreciate your enthusiasm and readiness to burn something down if we tell you to.

The first thing that you need to realize about stove is it does not have a simple On-Off switch, like your schlong. It's got a range of heat, from low to high. Most asshats[1] simply turn on the switch and start thinking this is cooking. NO! You need to control the heat, flame-boy. Start with medium heat on most dishes. If you're boiling water, or you are paying VERY close attention, you can get it on and crank the fire all the way up. Otherwise, keep it down, tiger. If you have a kick-ass stove like we do that throws fire like a Flammenwerfer, seriously, turn it DOWN. That's a flamethrower for you sensitive types.

Those sad people out there that have stoves with no actual fire, well, take heart; even though you don't have FIRE, you can make do. The electric "range top" is an embarrassment of society. They take time to heat up, can't cool down rapidly, and generally suck. If your stove is one of the sheets of glass with little pictures on it rather than words, and no dials, and has a little control panel like an iPod, then you are just going to have to practice your cooking until you can get women's collective opinion of you back up to "manly."

This is how we rank cooktops:
1) Gas fire and or gas with grill (the tools man is intended to cook with)
2) Induction - supposedly nice if you can get it (it is always nice to get it), but requires steel/iron cookware
3) Electric - sucks raw sheep testicles
4) Glass thing with no knobs - sucks raw goat[2] testicles sautéed in snail slime.

---

[1] a technical term
[2] Don't ask us why goat nuts rank lower than sheep. It is just the natural order of things

If you have one of the lesser cooktops, the best you can do is cook at whatever heat the recipe calls for, and be ready to yank the pan off the heat if things get too hot, until the burner backs down. Rumor has it you can also use the second burner, set to a lower temperature setting.[3]

The Microwave

Fire was discovered by man, and mastered in the form of the gas stove and grill. The electric range has to be so much better than the gas stove, right? Wrong. Nasty things. So too with the microwave; we don't really use it if we can avoid it. Too much rubber chicken and mushy veggies. We do melt things and boil water, and, of course, we do occasionally heat maple syrup or honey in the nukie for things that need warm syrup drizzled on them. Truthfully, the microwave is a good tool, but it is an add-on you can often do without.

Work it out in a real pot over real fire (FIRE! FIRE! FIRE!) if you can, Beavis.

Attitude and Measurements

A word about measurements. 36-24-36? Why yes, that IS nice, but not really the point just now. Neither is that other measurement that's on your mind. Put your junk away, pull your pants up, and get rid of that measuring tape. You are too easily distracted. If you've gotten this far, we figure you've got game, but we really don't want to think about your junk.

We sometimes will give you measurements in this book. Measurements like one cup, one teaspoon (the little one), one tablespoon (the big one), and so on, but what we really prefer when it comes to measurements…

DON'T.

Okay, occasionally do, but keep in mind that cooking is somewhat flexible. Measuring is for pastry chefs and other anal-retentive freaks of nature. We kid the pastry chefs. Even if they do make silly things like cupcakes. No really, we love pastry chefs, we just don't want to BE one. We want to be cooks.

Cooks can take five handfuls of ingredients and with nothing more than their calibrated fingers and knife-scarred hands, create culinary[4] sex. For example, if you don't have a teaspoon handy, use your cupped hand and estimate it. If a recipe says 1/8 teaspoon salt, think, "That's about a pinch." Capiche?

---

[3] Props to buddy Scot Mathis for the electric stove pro-tip.
[4] "Culinary" means "related to kitchen or cooking."

MEASUREMENTS FOR MEN

Dash	One light shake from a shaker bottle. Also faster than a walk, but slower than a run.
Smidgin	Less than a pinch but more than a dash.
Pinch	1/8 teaspoon. If we catch you measuring that, we'll disown you. It's a literal pinch between the fingers, usually a spice.
Quickie	Sorry, wrong list.
Sprig	A small twig from a plant, such as an herb.
Scosche	A small amount, e.g., "A scosche of bullshit."
Handful	Literally, a handful. If you have unusually large hands, well done.
Firkin	9 gallons. Also a useful nickname for an asshat, in refined company.
Heaping	Similar to heaving, but in this case, a cup or spoonful that overflows the cup or spoon. A heaping breast is not usually how it's used, but we'll allow it.

This is your kitchen; you are the king of the pot, whisk, and especially the knife. Don't venture in here like a serf seeking a favor from Her Highness. Gently shoo her out of the kitchen. If you buy the food and clean up the mess, then it's your kitchen too, so do what Frankie says and *Relax*. Enter your new domain. Enjoy.

> **Tip:** Give in to temptation. Asceticism is for monks.

If you take something tasty and add another tasty thing, it's got a decent chance of being delicious. It won't be perfect the first time - hell it probably won't be *perfect* the hundredth time - but it will be probably be edible the first time, more or less. You will learn what you like, and also how to screw around with recipes. After a few run-throughs of most of our recipes, you will slip past most restaurant food into cheesy, meaty goodness.

Oh. It turns out your parents were wrong. Play with your food. Add more pepper. Toss in an onion. Grab that left over cheese and melt it onto your egg and toast. Taste it. Tweak it. Taste it again. Oh, and don't forget the bacon. Never, ever forget the bacon.

Knife Skillz

If you want to grow up and be a butter-slinging, balls-out, cooking badass, you are going to need a real knife. No, you're not Dundee; his knife was a little TOO badass for the kitchen. You want the knife to say this on the box: 8-inch chef's knife. Not 7-inch, not 9-inch. Eight. Got it?

Diaper Monkey:

We recommend either Wusthof or Shun. German steel and Samurai swords, need we say more? There is no comparison. If you must get a cheaper knife, you really should at least test-drive a Wusthof and feel how delectably it fits in your hand. See how it curves around your hand and feels balanced? How it warms to the touch? Notice the urge to yell "There can be only ONE!" That's what you want the chef's knife to feel like. You're gonna use it. A LOT.

If you just can't spring for the Wusthof, fall back on the trusty multipurpose Swiss Army knife and get yourself a Victorinox 8-inch, if you please.

This is your man stick.[5] Yeah, we said it. Treat it well! It needs to be SHARP, diaper monkey. A dull knife is like a limp dick. Useless. We will not

---

[5] "This is my rifle, this is my gun. One is for killin', the other for fun."

4

go into how to sharpen it here. Suffice it to say, if you don't know what you're doing, take your knife to be sharpened by a pro. Make sure the pro knows that a German knife is sharpened at a different angle than a Japanese knife. Fine cooking stores sell and sharpen knives for a small fee.

Knife skillz are a little too much to get into here without a video to help demonstrate them, so go to our website: www.manmeetsstove.com/videoz and click on the "Knife Skillz" video. Everything you need to know to be sufficiently dangerous will be given unto you.

Be SAFE. Remember the CLAW. Real chefs cut themselves, but you really don't NEED to.

Al Dente

Yeah, there's another one of those Frenchie words. So sorry to upset your Yankee-Spankee sensitivities but the French have been doing this crap for a long time, and the Italians would argue that they have been doing it for longer than that. Do not get between them unless your name is Bonaparte.

You need to focus on two things: heat, and time. Time and heat are our friends, but your enemies, Napoleon, because you have not yet learned. We are here to learn you.

As we mentioned in the Stove section, you need to control your fire. When in doubt turn it DOWN, you can get it up later.[6] You also need to be aware of how time affects your food. Example: Let's say you are looking at a picture of say, Kim Kardashian, in a compromised position. If you are careful and control your flame precisely, you can enjoy viewing Kim's assets for quite a long time. If you don't pace yourself, you can overheat, go short, and end up limp with very little to show for it.

If you can let go of the thought of Kim K., imagine your vegetables or pasta as your manhood. If you are careful with the heat, and limit the time, you will not end up with a limp product. This non-limp state is known as Al Dente. While you are cooking your vegetables or pasta, you need to occasionally reach in with a spoon and extract a piece to taste. In the case of pasta, if the pasta is still the same color yellow (or whatever) as when you started, not done enough. If it is half white, half yellow, you are getting close, taste it. That's still not done, right? Keep cooking, but check more often. When the pasta has bite, but is not like hard or brittle pasta, pull that pot off the fire and pour the pasta into a colander.[7] Do NOT wash the pasta! Just shake out the water and let it cool naturally, but serve it as SOON as you can. If you do this right, the pasta will have snap, but will have also been cooked through, but not to the point of squishiness, or gods' forbid, sliminess.

As to vegetables, the idea is similar. If you have broccoli steaming, you will see the broccoli go from its natural green to a very bright green. This is called a "sweat," and when you see the broccoli reach a sweat, it's time to start tasting it occasionally. If it's too hard, it's not done. If it has a slightly snap when you bite through the stem, then it is time to colander it, like the pasta. If it is all mushy, you have shot your wad and wasted the broccoli. So sad.

Al dente is the way food should be. We cannot tell you how many "restaurants" we have eaten at that have pasty pasta, and slaughtered vegetables. Do NOT make their mistake.

---

[6] Consult your doctor if you're confused, or need little blue pills.
[7] The bowl full of little holes.

A Word about Ingredients

You need to cook, because you need to eat. Pizza in a box is quick and cheap when you are both. But now you are going to cook. Buy some food, cans, boxes, and yes, brave the end of the store and buy some fresh grown things. Doesn't really matter what; it's all good one way or another. There are a few times when a specific brand or type really makes a difference; most of the time, it does not.

Ingredients can really make the meal. In general, you want your ingredients like you want your women: fresh, natural, naked. Okay, maybe naked doesn't apply, yet; but it had to be said. The fresher your ingredients, the better. Do not use a canned vegetable when a real one is available. Do not use dry spices if you can afford or can grow living ones.

> **Tip:**
> If you can get diapers, deodorant, and motor oil where you get your food, you may want to find a farmer's market. Just sayin'.

Freshness is particularly true of meats. The best example of this is fish: if it smells fishy at all.....fuggetaboutit, seriously. Meats such as steak and roast, you can check on the label for the sell date. The meat should appear red, not brown, with the exception of pork which should be lighter pink. Meat should also spring back after you poke it. More on poking later...

In general, you get what you pay for. If you go to Whole Paycheck market and get grass fed, organic raised, hormone-free beef that was personally pampered by a busty blonde Swedish maid, well of course, the meat is just going to melt in your mouth. If you buy your meat out of the 97 cent store, well, your colon is not going to treat you well tomorrow. And that's if you're lucky.

Eggs you would think are pretty simple, right? Nyet, comrade. Like all other animal products its GIGO: garbage in, garbage out. It's the same thing; if you can get organic, farm fresh, hormone free eggs, go for it. If you can't, well, get a second job. One egg to rule them all.

As for organic vegetables? Well, yeah, they are better for the world and probably your health in some ways, but taste-wise, well, we honestly can't really tell the difference between many of the vegetables, organic or dripping in pesticide. A potato of another color will smell just the same if you slather it in butter. There are, again, exceptions. Tomatoes are best if they are "heirloom" and picked ripe from the vine. Period. Don't even think about arguing with us.

Spices

He who controls the spices, controls the food. – Thomas and Jim

Some foods have good built-in flavor, such as steak, but many foods need added spices to make things pop. Think of spices as the bikini on a supermodel...or off the supermodel, if that's how you roll. I know it's how we do. But like scantily-clad women, spices have their models and then they have their supermodels. Fresh spices from your kitchen window or your back porch will simply blow your mind. The smell, the unusual flavors, the bright colors all draw you into the sex chamber of spicy goodness. So, if you want something done right, grow it yourself. No, don't grow that, that's illegal.[8]

Fresh spices from the store are not going to be as good as the ones you grow and pick, but if you can't roll your own, at least buy your main flavor ingredients fresh whenever you can.

---

[8] for now...

Dried spices offer up the advantage of a grand selection, ease of storage, and many flavors from around the world, but they don't keep forever, and they are like a freshly neutered dog - still a dog, but half the spirit. Dried spices lose their potency and there is no little blue pill for it. The complex layers of spice flavor will fade away the longer it sits on the shelf. As a rule, toss out ground up dried spices every year (we empty the old ones into the compost heap); whole spices in good containers keep for twice as long - two years for those of you that were overheating working out the math. Any spice that you can get whole, get whole. Grind. Grind. Grind it yourself.

What should be on your shelf to get started?

Basil	Oregano	Rosemary	Sage
Cumin	Chili Powder	Garlic Salt	Bay Leaf
Paprika	Thyme	Red Pepper Flakes	Mustard Powder

Those are our go-to spices. The following are good for sweet recipes, such as pumpkin pie and cookies:

Nutmeg	Cinnamon	Clove	Ginger Powder	Vanilla Beans (extract if you must)

Salt and Pepper

Salt and pepper have really evolved from your Grandma's poodle-shaped salt shaker with iodine-laced table salt and pre-ground pepper in a square spice can. A jog through the local grocery store can usually yield at least coarse Kosher Salt, and perhaps exotic varieties such as Himalayan Pink Salt (our personal fave). Your grocer may even have coarse sea salts, and perhaps a smoked salt, or maybe even a red or black salt from Hawaii.

Black pepper is on every table, everywhere, for a reason. It adds its special bite to about any savory dish one would want to consume, and some dishes such as Peppercorn Steak (recipe below) make pepper the entire show. Historically, black pepper was as valuable as gold and was even part of the ransom of Rome when it was sacked in 410 c.e. by the Goths. Who knew Goths had such good taste?

If you are still getting your pepper out of a can, just STOP. Go get a pepper mill (grinder) loaded with black pepper already. Why are you still reading this? Okay, you can leave after you finish this chapter.

Pepper is one of the key ingredients in meat spice rubs, the go-to spice to dress a salad, and some people even use it in desserts like ice cream, or lime and pepper cookies, or even to flavor one's espresso (if you're Italian). Go figure.

If you are going to be using black pepper as a main ingredient, Indian Tellicherry peppercorns are the preferred type to buy. If you are just using pepper in small amounts, regular peppercorns will suffice. That pre-ground canned crap needs to be recycled as an art project or something.

Go get that peppercorn mill!

Bacon, the Other Spice.

Bacon is pork belly that is salt-cured and smoked into what is typically a key breakfast meat. Prepare some eggs, some bacon, and some sourdough toast, plate it all up, and you have a fine start to the day. Tasty grub indeed, and what we eat when the vegetarians are far, far away. As you probably know, bacon has become the Supermodel of Foods™ as of late. It is found in everything from donuts to candy bars to ice cream. We wholeheartedly endorse this development. We think of bacon as "the other spice." If you fry bacon hard and crispy, then bash it with the back of your knife, you'll have a salad garnish or a salty sprinkle for the tops of your deviled eggs, ice cream, brownies, whatever. Use your imagination. If all else fails, try it on a Supermodel.

If you fry the bacon "just barely," you can add it to a sandwich or bake it into cornbread muffins for a little southern comfort.[9] Bacon also serves as the "moist maker," and can be used to lubricate foods. For example, corn-on-the-cob wrapped in bacon and tinfoil, then grilled, is one of life's more erotic moments. There are several meats that are better when grilled and wrapped in bacon, e.g., Filet Mignon, but we'll tell you more about that in the Meat section. Patience there, Skippy.

If you just need some quick bacon after reading this section, we recommend a Mango Kabob. Bacon, mango, bacon, onion, bacon, beef, bacon, onion, bacon, mango. Mango is optional. Grill.[10]

Oils and Other Lubricants

A word about oils. No, not 40 weight Valvolube, we are talking cooking oils here. There really are only two kinds of oil, in our opinion.

Some oils have the ability to take lots of heat and are used for things like deep frying. You know, food such as deep-fried chicken from the Colonel, French fries, chicken nuggets, and other forms of heart-attack-in-a-tub. Yes, we understand, we eat the crap too. These oils include corn oil, peanut oil, and sesame oils. We prefer Grapeseed Oil, although it is not quite as heat tolerant. For day-to-day cooking, we recommend Extra Virgin Olive Oil (which we will refer throughout the book as olive oil) as it is simply better tasting, healthier, and uses the word "virgin." Enough said.

Stuff You Should Have on Hand by the Cutting Board

White wine
Red Wine
Red Wine Vinegar
Balsamic Vinegar
Rice Vinegar
Tarragon Vinegar (do you see a theme here?)
Pink Himalayan Rock Salt (because who doesn't like pink?)
Chicken and Beef Bullion
Garlic Oil
Spicy Hot Pepper Oil
Extra Virgin Olive Oil (our go-to oil for most things)
Grapeseed / Canola Oil (you need one oil with a very light taste that you can heat really hot)

Dried Oregano
Dried Italian Blend Seasoning
Black Pepper in Grinder
Garlic Salt / Garlic Powder
Onion Salt / Powder
Rooster "Cock" Sauce
Worcestershire Sauce
Sambal Alek Red Pepper Sauce
Grey Poupon Mustard
Cilantro Oil

Hot Peppers

While you are out gathering spices, you really must get some; not that, we mean hot peppers. As Real Men™ we know you'll be shopping from the bottom of the Scoville Unit table on the next page. Wilbur Scoville came up with a scientific test to measure hotness[11] by diluting pepper extract with sugar syrup until a panel of five people couldn't taste the pepper. The more sugar syrup needed, the hotter the pepper. 15 million is "pure" heat. Pepper spray is an average 4.5 million Scoville Units. Pepper heat, while important, can actually make food unpleasant to eat, so if you want to impress her, you may want to focus more on the flavor of the pepper and less on competing with your buddy's ability to drink shots of "Scorched Ass Hot Sauce." If you use anything hotter than a Scotch Bonnet, you deserve to be shot for excessive dick waving. Flavor is found towards the top of the

---

[9] You might actually want Southern Comfort, either type, with this...
[10] Nosh.
[11] Measuring hotness in women, requires eyes and a review of the Periodic Table of Hotness.

chart. We roll with Thai peppers, but then we are trained professionals. You should stick to Bells. Remember it's not the heat, it's the humidity.

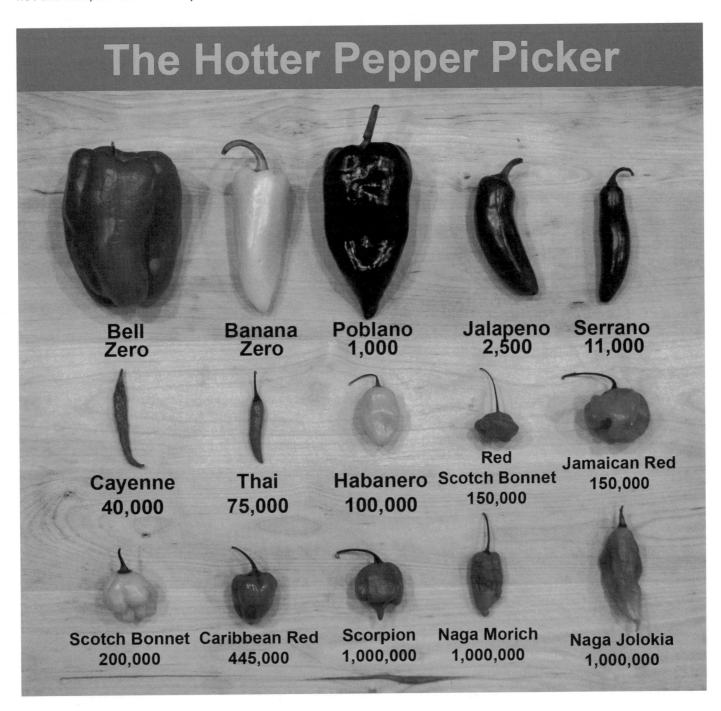

The Hotter Pepper Picker

Bell Zero	**Banana** Zero	**Poblano** 1,000	**Jalapeno** 2,500	**Serrano** 11,000
Cayenne 40,000	**Thai** 75,000	**Habanero** 100,000	**Red Scotch Bonnet** 150,000	**Jamaican Red** 150,000
Scotch Bonnet 200,000	**Caribbean Red** 445,000	**Scorpion** 1,000,000	**Naga Morich** 1,000,000	**Naga Jolokia** 1,000,000

Cracking Eggs. No, Not a Shot to the Balls.

There are essentially two schools of thought on cracking eggs: our school, and the wrong school. Okay, we kid; the two schools of crack are: 1) cracking on a flat surface like the counter, or 2) cracking the eggs on the rim of the bowl you're about to put them in. Oh, just go watch the video at www.manmeetsstove.com/videoz and click on the Cracking Eggz video.

If you are cracking on the flat, take the egg in your dominant hand (that's the one you polish your knob with), and tap the egg so it makes a small dent in the side of the egg. Over a bowl, turn the egg so the dent is up, and using both hands on each side of the egg, pull the dent rim apart, splitting the egg in two halves and dumping the contents in the bowl.

If you are cracking on the rim of the bowl, again, take the egg in your dominant hand (that's the one you spank her ass with) and crack the egg on the rim, turn it slightly, and crack it again. This technique is one-handed. With the egg cupped in your hand, you can hold onto one end of the egg with your pinkie and ring-finger. Use your forefinger and thumb to pinch the other end of the egg and pull the two halves apart. Yeah, go watch the video. If you want, you can also use the two handed technique[12] to open the egg after you crack it on the rim as well.

> **Tip:**
> Don't put too much stock in experts.
> Except us, of course.

If any pieces of shell go into the bowl: FAIL. No, relax, it's no biggie; fish 'em out with one of the eggshell halves, a spoon, or your clean fingers (which you have washed thoroughly after polishing your knob OR spanking her ass). If you practice enough, and you will, you'll get comfortable with whatever technique you choose and you will mock lesser beings that can't do it your way, since it IS the correct way.

Sanitation

Wash your damn hands. With soap and HOT water. For more than 20 seconds.[13] If you are too delicate for HOT water, grow a pair and develop some calluses. Repeat often. 'Nuff said. This applies to many things. If you want to get into her lunch box, you better not smell like an orangutan.[14]

Bacteria and other Kitchen Transmitted Diseases (KTDs)[15]

There are few things more vile than poultry when it comes to bacteria. Chickens are like Zombies; if they infect you, you're single for life.[16] When handling chicken, think of yourself as being in the Radioactive Hot Zone (like Japan after a quake), and everything you touch becomes infected. Your hands, the knife, the cutting board, etc., etc. When dealing with chicken, or any meat really, the trick is proper layout of the work area of your kitchen. Don't be a slob. Have a second cutting board, just for your meat, and place it by itself next to the sink. If you're working with a whole chicken, pull out the giblets (liver, heart, neck) from inside the body cavity of the chicken. The nice butcher leaves those in there for a reason. Put the giblets[17] in a bowl. Wash the chicken inside and out, pat dry with a paper towel, throw away the towel immediately, and then set the chicken on the board. Do what you need to do with the chicken: apply a rub, cut it up, whatever; paying close attention not to contaminate any extra poultry rub in the container, veggies, whatever, with your hands or the chicken. Put the chicken into the pan or pot. Then it's decontamination time. Wash that shit DOWN. Cutting board into the sink. Soap the hell out of it. Wash your hands. Carefully clean your cutting knife with a soapy sponge, whatever you do, don't cut yourself while washing it. Wash your hands. Wash anything else the chicken or its juices might have touched: counter, faucet, whatever. One more time, wash your hands. Capiche?

---

[12] Remember, two hands can chafe.
[13] ....if you think that 20 seconds is too long you've already got a major problem.
[14] No orangutans were harmed in the making of this joke.
[15] Not to be confused with STDs which one gets from unprotected sex on the kitchen table, counter, and floors
[16] Okay, maybe not for life, but she won't want to be anywhere near your bad plumbing for a good long while
[17] Giblets are also known as "offal," the internal organs of an animal. They are, in fact, NOT awful. Quite tasty, in fact.

Cutting Boards

Cutting boards are like ammunition for your gun. No, not that gun, meathead - your firearm. They can literally make or break your knife while you are cutting, chopping, dicing, and slicing. A dull knife is like a broken sewer, it can't move shit.

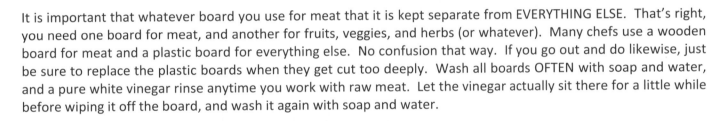

There is a great debate in the culinary world as to plastic or wood, but there is no debate about glass, stone, or metal cutting boards. Fuggetaboutit. Take glass, metal, or stone cutting boards and take them out for target practice. Use them for smacking someone upside...no don't do that, we are not advocates of violence...much. No, there are only two options: wood, and plastic. WHY? Because we are trying to kill bacteria, and not dull the crap out of our knife in the process.

The government actually requires that plastic be used in food outfits like restaurants. However, Pointy-Headed Scientists™ conducted studies[18] and discovered that wood cutting boards have natural anti-bacterial properties and, even better, are somewhat self-repairing from the cuts of the knife. On the other hand, plastic can be easily disinfected with a good soap and hot water wash, but bacterial critters can hide in deep cuts of the plastic, so wash well.

It is important that whatever board you use for meat that it is kept separate from EVERYTHING ELSE. That's right, you need one board for meat, and another for fruits, veggies, and herbs (or whatever). Many chefs use a wooden board for meat and a plastic board for everything else. No confusion that way. If you go out and do likewise, just be sure to replace the plastic boards when they get cut too deeply. Wash all boards OFTEN with soap and water, and a pure white vinegar rinse anytime you work with raw meat. Let the vinegar actually sit there for a little while before wiping it off the board, and wash it again with soap and water.

There are many kinds of plastic and wood boards out there. Here's our advice - get a hardwood "endgrain" wood board. John Boos cutting boards are the best, in our opinion. Do not get a thin softwood board such as pine

wood. Soft woods WILL warp when they get really wet, plus your Shun blade will cut right through it.[19]

It helps if your plastic board has some kind of sticking feet.[20] If you want to be an overachiever in the wood department, and what guy doesn't, you can get a board for each occasion: beef, poultry, vegetables, small cutting jobs, etc. Just be sure to clean them regularly, and especially after poultry. A little botulism amongst friends might kill you.

It is true what they say, bigger IS better. We like cutting boards about an inch thick and 18 by 20 inches in size. That being said, you will need to have a decent-sized kitchen, and sink, for that mondo board. You will need

---

[18] The ironically named Dr. Dean O. Cliver, if you are interested in Googling the geeky white paper.

[19] Not really

[20] If you have a really well-endowed big cutting board like us, you won't need to worry about it moving on you.

to choose your boards to fit your kitchen and sink because you are going to be washing your boards often in your kitchen, not ours. One last reminder: always sport clean gear; wash your wood often.

Tools (You Knew There Was Gear, Didn't You?)

A famous chef by the name of Alton Brown has a strict rule that says NO to kitchen tools that only have one use.[21] There are, however, exceptions. That being said, you don't have to go out and buy every tool that looks shiny, lest you BE a tool. If you don't have all of the following things….it's okay! Improvise, soldier! But this is a good list if you are going on a gear spree:

Big frying pan – nonstick
Little frying pan – nonstick
Small boiling pot – nonstick
Large stew pot – ceramic coated iron or aluminum
Colander
Waffle Maker
Rice cooker
Tongs
Steamer basket or electric steamer
Immersion/stick blender (we like to blend)

Box grater (a sturdy one)
8-inch chef's knife
3-inch paring (peeling) knife
Serrated tomato knife
Cutting blocks (one plastic, one wood, see above)
Wooden spoons/scrapers (hardwood preferred)
Veggie peeler
Nested mixing bowls
Digital instant-read thermometer
Citrus squeezer

One unitasker we make an exception for is an orange/lemon squeezer. We prefer the style that looks like a pair of orange pliers. If you are just squeezing one citrus fruit like a lemon, simply cut the lemon in half and squeeze each half over your cupped hand. Let the juice dribble through your cupped hand[22] into a glass, but keep your fingers just together enough that the lemon seeds stay in your hand.

Rice cookers have advanced to such a degree that you can put whatever rice you like into it, add the recommended water and push a button that corresponds to the type of rice. If you've got money to blow, get a Zojirushi rice cooker and rock on, rich man. If you're like us, get a cheaper model that holds enough rice for you and that woman we're trying to help you bed. Like a good missile (and unlike trying to cook rice on the stove), a rice cooker is "fire and forget."

If we catch you buying a mango de-seeder, spaghetti fork, apple slicer/peeler/corer, or a Yoni[23] banana ice cream maker, we're gonna have to have a talk with Cousin Guido about your tool problem. You don't want to meet Cousin Guido…

---

[21] Also known as "unitaskers." Mango Seed Hair Cleaners really aren't necessary; use your tongue.
[22] Insert your own punchline here. We got brainlocked with the potential.
[23] Your woman has a Yoni for your banana. You shouldn't have to buy one.

easy[24]

We're gonna try to start you off like the virgin you probably are. We'll be gentle. We know you probably can't so much as boil water yet, but follow the instructions, experiment, burn shit up, and maybe even blow up a few things. We'll have you cooking for that woman in no time.

Jet Fuel for the Revolution

Soundtrack: Uh! All Night by KISS

You may be young enough to keep it up for Miss November...however, you gotta keep that brain active while you do it. She's seen it all, and a woman that fine is gonna require some tricks. You are going to need coffee, stud, and lots of it.

We are guessing you have a machine that involves a filter paper, a glass carafe, and button pushing. No. Step away, Mister Coffee. We're gonna teach you how to make DECENT coffee, something that will impress the ladies, not that swill you've been throwing down your gullet at work.

First, you're going to need to buy some gear. Yes, really. The "gear" is known as a French press, or a Press Pot. We call it a French Press because we know that despite their reputation as cheese-eating surrender monkeys, the French also know how to impress the ladies, with or without food, and well, they eat cheese. Fine cheese. REALLY fine cheese.

The other gear you're gonna need is a coffee grinder. Before you get all creative and try to grind your coffee using a V8 powered driver drill or cement mixer, we are looking for a particular KIND of coffee grinder, specifically a Burr Grinder. Do NOT buy a blade grinder, grunt. They chop the coffee and make a mess of it. They are inconsistent crap. The French Press and Burr Grinder should set you back less than $50. As with all gear, you can spend a LOT more than that, if you want to. Knock yourself out, moneybags, but a suave man knows where to spend and where to save (socks, for instance).

> **Tip:**
> If you want to live, don't touch the chef's coffee.

Go out and purchase some good coffee. No, not that crap-in-a-can. Buy the coffee by the bean, whole. Pre-ground coffee is like opening her double-E bra to find tissue paper filler. It's just not right.

Coffee from Central and South America tend to be mild, which they refer to as "Light Bodied." Think Natalie Portman. African and Middle Eastern beans are medium-bodied and medium acidity. Think Halle Berry. Beans from Indonesia and the Islands like Hawaii are heavy-bodied with low acidity, and are earthy, like Christina Hendricks.

Coffee bean selection is, of course, way more complicated than that, but this is a start. Buy your beans and pour them in the burr grinder, set it to coarse grind, and grind away. You will need two tablespoons of ground coffee for each cup of water. More coffee if you're a man's man. Place the ground coffee into the bottom of the French press.

---

[24] Easy food, like women, can still be tasty.

Your coffee is only as good as the water you put in it. If your tap water tastes like a pissed-in public swimming pool, you're going to want to get filtered water, or something that only has deer piss in it, like mountain spring water. Heat the water by whatever means you have. An electric pot is great; over a stove is fine too.

Pour a little bit of your good, hot water into the French Press with the ground coffee.[25] Pour it slowly, so as to saturate the coffee evenly, and then wait. You should see the coffee expand and foam up. This is actually air[26] releasing from the coffee. A coffee fart. When the coffee grounds have finished expanding, pour in the rest of the water.

Orchids are our favorite flower.

Think hard.

Set a timer to four minutes. After one minute, stir the water and coffee grounds in the French press with a spoon and let it settle again. Just before four minutes, place the lid onto the French press, making sure to line up the drain in the cap with the pour spout, with the press retracted all the way up. At four minutes, push the press down. SLOWLY, minute-man. Take 30 seconds to push it all the way in. Slowly. Think of it as a virgin. The press should gently push the coffee grounds to the bottom.

When the coffee grounds are pressed, pour the coffee immediately into cups. If you have any coffee leftover in the French press, do NOT leave it there. It will get nasty, fast. If you have selected a coffee that is bitter, or it tastes too bitter to you anyway, add a pinch of salt to it. No, really. Salt makes things taste good, right? It may help. Try it. Just a pinch. Non-flavored gourmet salt or Kosher salt, if you've got it.

If you want to try some other coffee machines, the Chemex, Melitta, Café Solo, and vacuum pots all make a good cuppa Joe. If you really want the best, Comrade, espresso is for you, and you can even use a stovetop espresso maker to do it on the cheap. We'll have a latte, thanks. Shaken, not stirred.

Go find Miss November and give her some of that brew, maybe with a bite of chocolate. Those supermodel-types usually don't eat much, but then, hey, they have other redeeming qualities.

Ramen Noodles Done Right

Soundtrack: *Big in Japan* by Alphaville

2 Packages Ramen Noodles

Optional Accessories:

Spicy Oil	Chicken Bullion	Nori Seaweed
Miso Soup Paste	Egg	Bean Sprouts
Cabbage	Sausage	Corn
Butter!	Parmesan Cheese	

Having once been locked up in a boarding school for months at a time, we appreciate the fine art of eating Ramen noodles. No really, we've tried it ALL, including taking the Ramen noodles and opening the bag, opening the spice packet and throwing it in, closing the bag, pounding the dry ramen into little bits with a fist, and eating the crunchy seasoned bits out of the bag, like potato chips. We do not recommend this for untrained professionals.

Yes, that would be you.

---

[25] Remember: two tablespoons of ground coffee for each cup of water.
[26] *GEEK ALERT* Actually, carbon dioxide.

We do recommend that you learn to cook ramen perfectly. That's right; there IS a way to jack it up, and it is called overcooking-the-noodles-to-slime. Nobody wants that, so here's what you do.

Heat a small pot of water to boiling on high heat. We prefer to have just enough water to barely cover the two ramen bricks when placed into the pot, but if you like the broth, follow the directions on the package. When the water is boiling, put the ramen bricks into the water, one on top of the other. Throw in the flavor packets. (Be sure to open the actual packets and dump spices into the water; hint, hint.)

After a minute or so, turn the bottom brick to the top with a wooden spoon or spatula, and repeat the flip again a little bit later so both bricks keep getting heated evenly. Keep rotating the bricks and watch for them to start separating into noodles. Help them with that, but not so that you break the noodles into little bits.

When the noodles start to separate, start watching them carefully. When you started, they were kind of a white color. As you cook them, you will see the noodles turn from white to a more yellow color that is slightly see-through.[27] When you see the noodles start to turn soft, take a noodle out and taste it. It's probably still hard and not tasty. Okay, stir the noodles up, and wait for about 30 seconds. Taste a noodle again. A little less brittle? No? Stir for another 30 seconds.

At some point the noodles are going to be kinda soft, but not so soft that they are overcooked, slimy nastiness. Immediately remove them from the fire and pour into a bowl. If they are still slightly firm, it's okay, they will still cook in the bowl for a little bit. The trick is to remove them well BEFORE they go slimy. Al dente[28] is what you are shooting for.

If you jack it up, throw it away! Ramen are like 20 cents, right? There is no excuse for bad ramen.

Here's the fun part. As the ratchet wranglers would say, it's time to add the turbo.

Spicy oil is an absolute no-brainer. Some real Japanese ramen noodles even come with a packet included. Just pour in a half a teaspoon or more and nosh away if you're a badass. If you like a little more flavor than the packets provide, add a little chicken bouillon to taste.

Nori Seaweed is available at most grocery stores in the Asian food section near the fancy ramens. Nori is the wrapper that goes on the outside of those "California rolls" some simpleton folk call sushi.[29] Just toss a couple of seaweed squares into the soup while it's hot, and it will wilt and add a tasty change of pace.

Miso soup paste is what makes the soup that they serve you at sushi joints. It's very salty and flavorful, so you will want to only use one of the ramen spice packets, or none, while cooking the soup, and add just a little miso paste to the soup to taste a little bit at a time. Go easy lest you blow up the soup with salty miso flavor.

Egg and cabbage are options that can be added earlier in the cooking process as they need to cook. Just dump the egg and/or cabbage after you've cooked the ramen bricks a little. Bean sprouts can be added during the latter part of the cooking process, or after, for a little crunch.

Sausage. What else needs to be said? Dice it up and throw it in after the ramen is done.

Corn. Yeah, probably half a can of corn will do. Add it at the end of the cooking.

---

[27] Like a good nightie.
[28] "Al dente" means "to the bite" in Italian. It means firm, but not hard. Unlike what you want to be when in bed with Katy Perry.
[29] The same people that think French Fries are from France, and that healthy fish taco tastes fishy.

Butter! Again, what else needs to be said? A pat or two will do ya. Add during cooking. Yum.

Parmesan Cheese. Oh baby, how we love thee. We sometimes say there is only one reason to buy that crap parmesan cheese in a plastic bottle and that's for popcorn. We lied. You can use it here, too. It is, after all, ramen. Dump some parmesan in near the end of the cooking. Or if you happen to be cool like us, grate some real parmesan cheese instead and throw it in. Don't hold back now!

Fried. Yes, fried. If you are going to fry some ramen noodles to go with your meat, you need to follow the directions above for cooking the noodles, only this time take them off the heat even EARLIER. You don't want them crispy, but they shouldn't be edible either. Take the partially cooked noodles and throw them in a pan with a slight coating of olive oil. Because you know how you like things coated in oil. Anyway…cook the noodles in the frying pan, start by stirring them around a little with a wooden spoon, and then press them down into the pan kinda flat so they make a noodle pancake. Let them cook like that for a minute or so, then flip them over and do the same on the other side. Remove from the heat, and plate. Goes well with steak. But what doesn't?

Smack and Cheese

Soundtrack: *Things Can Only Get Better* by Howard Jones

2 Boxes Macaroni and Cheese

Heavy Cream	Cheddar Cheese	Monterey Jack Cheese
Cream Cheese	Black Pepper	Paprika
Chili Pepper	Basil	

You used to eat out of a box. We know it. You know it. She knows it.[30] This recipe will start the thought in that sexy mind of hers that maybe, just maybe, you know your way around the kitchen and perhaps promote you from being a distraction to a full-time occupation.

Follow the directions on the Crack and Cheese boxes, but substitute in heavy cream for the milk and use butter instead of margarine. When you are ready to pour in the magic cheese packet, pause; here's where the fun begins. Add in 1/4 block of cream cheese and a handful of the grated jack and cheddar cheeses. Stir. Taste. Think of that as the minimum dish. Add the spices a little tiny bit at a time, and taste it again. If you like the taste, stop. Add more spice and you might destroy it.

Enjoy.

About the leftovers, assuming there are any, your old self would just eat them cold with a can of caffeine-laced soda or with a can of warm cheap beer. Don't. This time you're gonna pull out a baking dish, sprinkle the bottom of the dish with the little broken bits of Doritos leftover from the bottom of the bags, grate some more cheese over that, and spread the leftover mac-n-cheez over the top of that. Grate some more cheese on the top and shake a manly portion of chili pepper and paprika over the top. Cover it and fridge it.

---

[30] She knows you love to eat out a box better than anyone. Hopefully.

Bake sometime during the next week for 25 minutes at 325° uncovered so the top gets brown and crunchy. Serve that up again and see if she keeps you around, or at least promotes you to a dinnertime booty call.

Ten Tacos

Soundtrack: *Puttin' on the Ritz* by Taco

The taco is yet another fine place to put your meat and cheese. The old saying that the clothes make the man, or in your case, man-child, is also true for your taco.[31] The tortilla makes the taco. If you can get homemade taco tortillas from a Mexican lass, you're one lucky man. Without a little senorita to service you, smoke your tires over to the grocery store and get some tortillas. You're looking for the 4-inch ones. They are small enough that if you start on a taco and don't like it, well, then it is over quick. A quickie, as it were.

The store should carry at least two kinds of taco tortilla, corn and flour. If you are fortunate to live near a market that has fresh flour tortillas, spring for 'em. They are really good. However, your regular tortillas in a plastic bag will do fine.

A word on heating a taco: remember the ladies need a lot more time than we do to get warmed up.[32] Take some time. As to heating a tortilla, well that goes a lot faster... If you are heating a flour tortilla, you can simply turn on a burner on the stove, grab a pair of tongs or a wooden spoon, and set a tortilla directly on the burner. Let it sit there for a few seconds, and flip it using the tongs or wooden spoon. Keep doing this. When you start to see little bubbles appearing in the tortilla, you're done. If you don't flip it fast enough and burn the tortilla, throw it away, no problem. Start another one, only flip it faster and remove it sooner. A little blackening is okay, you just don't want it to be a nuclear event.

If you're a corn tortilla fan like we are, you need to bust out a frying pan. Very lightly coat the pan with oil and let it heat up a little. Throw a tortilla in the pan and let it heat up for about 30 seconds. Flip it using a wooden spoon and let the other side cook until you see bubbles appear. If you want soft tacos, you're done. If you want crispy taco shells, flip it again and let it cook much longer, keep lifting the tortilla as it cooks, and when it gets to the point it is crispy, remove it from the pan and set it on a paper towel. Fold it in half and let it cool.

Almost anything can go into a taco from chorizo sausage to left-over mystery meat. Armed with your taco shells, start with the basic taco elements. You can grate just about any cheese you like, including something hot like pepper-Havarti, or smooth like Monterey Jack. There doesn't need to be much, but the cheese mellows and blends the flavors. Sour cream is a traditional element, fresh, cool, and on top. Avocado slices are like a green sideways smile and bring smooth coolness to the mouth. Fresh tomato-onion-cilantro salsa[33] from the deli section of your grocery store is really good. Hot sauce out of the packet or the jar brings more heat, and a bonus of flavor and perceived fearlessness in her mind. Hot sauce has become a gourmet item and the varieties are limitless. You can select from green (mild to medium hot), red (mild to deathly hot), habañero (you'll-wish-you-were-dead hot), to chipotle (smoky). If you can take the heat, check out the Hmong Salsa on page 23. We like 'em all. Okay, maybe we could do without the habañero. It really is that hot.

We think you are ready, so follow along closely. These are all just starting points; embellish as your taste guides you.

---

[31] Or her's, as the case may actually be.
[32] 20 minutes on average, dude. Yes, seriously.
[33] Also called Pico de Gallo or Salsa Fresca

Ground beef taco - Get some ground beef from your grocer. Do NOT get anything less than 20% fat (known as 80/20); otherwise, it is tasteless. The package should state the fat content clearly. Remove the burger from the package, place it on your cutting board, and use your fingers to mix a little fresh ground black pepper, paprika, chopped fresh garlic,[34] and red pepper flakes into the ground beef. Turn on the fire under a frying pan and crumble the beef into the pan with your fingers, stirring occasionally with a wooden spoon. Break up any clumps that form, as you'll want the cheese and other goodies to get all around the cooked hamburger. Throw in a pinch or two of salt while cooking. When the burger is cooked to a fairly even brown, place about an inch of burger, a bit of grated cheese, a little chopped onion, and a pinch of fresh cilantro into each taco shell. Add the other ingredients such as salsa, hot sauce, and sour cream. Now if your girl is griping about your health, show a little shredded lettuce to the taco, for roughage. Just fail to mention the fatty burger to her. Add a slice of avocado. Enjoy.

Chicken taco – Go to your grocer and get a pre-cooked boneless chicken, or grab some left over Colonel's chicken, cut the chicken off the bone into small bites, and toss them into the little frying pan with butter or olive oil, a squeeze of lime, rosemary sprig (fresh preferred), and a few spoonfuls of salsa. When the chicken bits are heated, remove, and place equally into the taco shells. Cover with a little sour cream or ranch dressing, and add a bit of shredded cabbage or lettuce to the top.

Vegehuvian – This taco requires a broiler in your oven. No, that is not an expression. At the bottom of your stove, under the oven, is a smaller door with a drawer that slides out. That is the broiler, not convenient pull-out storage. If you don't have one, skip this recipe. If you do have a broiler, start by cooking up a batch of white or brown rice in your rice cooker. When the rice is done, heat up a can o' beans (black or pinto) in a pot, or even nuke them in a bowl in the microwave. Using a big plastic or wooden spoon, separate the beans and pour off the bean juice. Put the beans on flat prepared taco shells, then sprinkle on some rice. Get a pepper such as a Bell (super mild), Anaheim (mild), or Serrano (ass lighter). Slice the stem/top off the pepper and cut it open on one side and lay it out flat. Using your knife, scrape away the seeds and the white membrane stuff from the opened pepper. Cut the remaining flattened outside of the pepper into thin strips and lay them over the rice in the taco. Cover with slices of avocado and then sprinkle with

a mellow white cheese such as Monterey Jack. Place the tacos in or on an oven-safe dish or pan that fits in the broiler. Look at your knob - no, not that one, the one on your oven. It should have a "broil" or "broiler" setting. Turn it on. Open the broiler drawer and place your tacos inside the drawer, slide it back into the oven, and broil under the burners for about 60 seconds. Do NOT let them actually catch fire. That is not the kind of hot we're looking for. Open the broiler, using oven mitts, remove the pan of tacos, and serve.

Steak Taco - You tied one on at dinner last night, and along with a rippin' hangover, there is a doggie bag with left-over Prime Rib or New York steak in the fridge. It's taco time. Fix up some taco shells and then cover them with a thin layer of cream cheese. Lay in some slices of Pepper Jack cheese.[35] Thinly slice some onion, you will need it later. Pop the tacos briefly under the broiler to get them tan and toasty (see broiler instructions in Vegehuvian Taco section, above). Meanwhile, slice up the left-over steak into roughly ¼-inch slabs. Using oven mitts, pull your tacos out of the broiler, add the thinly sliced onions, and put them back under the broiler to get the onions

---

[34] ...or garlic powder if you must. NOT garlic salt.
[35] GEAR time! A cheese plane is a handy tool for this, if you got one. Or if you got a spare Washington or two to get one.

warmed up. Give the onions about 30 seconds, pull the tacos out again, and add the steak. Put the tacos back in the broiler one last time to heat up the steak, briefly. Using the oven mitts, remove the tacos and dress them with the following: two spoonfuls of sour cream and one spoonful of hot sauce that was well mixed with a few crushed and minced garlic cloves.[36]

Carne Asada - Grab the left over Carne Asada. Lay a couple of green onions (with the roots and tips) into the frying pan, add butter, and shake on some salt and black pepper.[37] Turn the onions when they smell good. Lay out the tacos while the Carne Asada heats up in a frying pan over low heat next to the green onions (add a bit more butter and salt to the green onions, don't overdo it), as the meat just needs to be warm enough to melt the cheese. Sprinkle some shredded Monterey Jack cheese over the taco shells, and flick a little fresh lime or orange juice onto the meat. Lay one green onion on each taco. Cover with the meat and add a slice of avocado. Add either a splash of balsamic or hot sauce.[38] Dealer's choice.

Porky Pig Taco - This is the "it" taco, men. Pork is another way the gods let us know we are as awesome as we are. Lay out the taco shells. Acquire, through generally legal means, ground pork from your local market. Dice half an onion (see www.manmeetsstove.com/videoz "Knife Skillz" video). Throw the onion into your frying pan (medium heat) with some olive oil and stir occasionally till the onions turn golden. Add the ground pork to the pan and smash to mix with onions and break up the pork. Cook 'til pork turns white and no pink is visible, or 160 degrees off a meat thermometer. Mash up a ripe avocado with a fork, add black pepper and salt, a little bit of mayo, sour crème, or crème fresca, and a splash of hot sauce. Mix together. Spread this Green Glop™ onto the shells, sprinkle with chopped onion and garlic, and add a few forkfuls of pork down the middle of each taco.

Turkey Taco - This is best served for the day-after-Thanksgiving lunch, but anytime you have access to fresh roasted turkey will do. Take a chunk of light and dark meat. Use your chef's knife and the wood block and cut it up into bites. Toss the meat in a medium frying pan and add some green chili. If you are using canned chilis pour the chilis in with the turkey, juice and all. Add some fresh cilantro and some chicken or turkey stock. Season the mix with black pepper. Heat the turkey up on medium-low flames; yeah, it is going to take a few minutes, so keep your knickers on. While that is heating up, set out a few taco tortillas and lay on a few thin slices of pepper jack cheese. Slice up an avocado into long, thin spears. Spoon out the turkey chunks and set them in rows on the cheese, and then butch the tacos up with the avocado spears and a few chopped tomatoes.

Shredded Chicken Taco - Take the leftovers of Chicken-Go-Pow from page 53, set out some taco shells, and spread them with a schmear of sour cream or crème fresca. Load up the taco shells with the chicken and fill it up with cut tomatoes and goat cheese. For a Cal-Mex chicken taco, spread a thin layer of canned spicy black bean dip on the taco shells. Load up the chicken on the beans and crumble on some farmers cheese.[39] Finish the Cal-Mex off with avocado and tomato tossed with olive oil, balsamic vinegar (optional), and black pepper.

Meat and Potatoes Taco - This barely qualifies as a Mexican dish. This is more of an "I have five items in my pathetic food box and I am not going out" sort of a deal. But it is tasty, if rather un-authentic and pathetic. When you have left over Roast Beast (see page 46), then set some aside for these tacos. Dice up a handful of whatever potato you have on hand, add the potato pieces to a pan, along with some olive oil, black pepper, and the good salt. Pour in enough beef stock to half cover them, lid it up, and let it ride on a 25% flame until a fork goes easily into the meat. Pull apart a few servings of the meat with two forks and put your meat and potatoes into the taco.[40]

---

[36] …or use garlic powder (not garlic salt), if you must.

[37] Do NOT dance while doing this, because no one wants to see that.

[38] Or add a flood of hot sauce if that's how you roll. You know we do.

[39] Farmer's Cheese is a mild white fresh cheese also known as "Queso Fresco" or "Ranchero" cheese.

[40] Insert your own punch line here.

Fish Tacos - We don't think you are up to this. Really. Instead, drive to Ensenada. Just past the tourista strip mall thingie and turn right, drive about two blocks and on the left is a hot turquoise and sun yellow building that has a big sign that says "FISH TACOS." That place is crap. Drive past that, and immediately on the left is a taco truck that has a sort of shack built over it. Walk up to the truck window, order three of anything,[41] and joyfully eat what they bring you. THAT is a Fish Taco.™ If you want to know how to make those at home you will have to buy our next book. Or move to Ensenada and get an apprenticeship.

Drunk Broccoli

Soundtrack: *Land of Confusion* by Genesis

2 Heads of broccoli	Olive oil	Partial bottle of wine
5 Cloves of garlic	Himalayan pink salt	

Optional: Hot pepper olive oil or red pepper flakes

Break out the broccoli and your big-ass 8-inch chef's knife. Very carefully cut the tops of the broccoli where the broccoli branches are about a ½ to ¼-inch thick. Those little broccoli heads are called "florets" because some French bastard thought they looked like a "little flower." Okay, so actually they ARE little flowers. Details, details, we kid the French.

Set aside but keep the thick stalks of the broccoli for the next recipe (see below).

Mash some garlic cloves with the flat of your knife blade (careful with that sharp edge, Bruce Lee) and remove the dry skin from the cloves. Cut the garlic cloves into thin slices. Bust out your big frying pan and throw in a generous amount of olive oil, your sliced garlic, and a pinch of salt. If you like it peppery (and who doesn't?), add the hot pepper oil now, or some red pepper flakes. Let it fry until it just starts to sizzle then carefully pour in a lot of wine[42] (stand back, hot oil will splatter when you add water or wine). Drop in the broccoli florets. Keep your florets moving[43] by occasionally stirring them with a wooden spoon, so they are well coated and evenly cooked in the boiling wine. After about seven minutes, grab one of the florets and taste it. It should have a little snap in the stem, but not too much (that "al dente" thing again; learn it). If the floret is too hard, cook for a little while longer. You do NOT want it squishy.[44] When the florets are al dente, remove from the fire, retrieve the broccoli from the wine with a spoon, and plate.

Man Broccoli
- Max Bork

Not everyone likes broccoli. Use this Drunk Broccoli to prove them wrong.

---

[41] Those prices are in pesos. To feed your entire herd of walking germ-bags will cost you about $5 U.S.
[42] ...but not a firkin.
[43] That is not a dance move
[44] That is kind of a metaphor for life, really.

Broccoli Soup

Stalks from the Drunk Broccoli recipe (see above)
Sour cream
Ground Himalayan pink salt
Garlic powder

1 can Cream of Chicken soup
Butter
Fresh ground pepper
Optional: Extra sharp cheddar cheese

Peel the broccoli stalks with a potato peeler or a paring knife (BE CAREFUL! You're NOT a samurai, yet). If you don't have a hand blender, dice or mince the peeled broccoli stalks into very, very fine pieces (think grains of rice as a size reference). Remember, use your knife skills (www.manmeetsstove.com/videoz and click on "Knife Skillz" video). To cut them this fine, cut the stalks lengthwise with the tip of your 8-inch macho knife to form very thin stalk strips, and then turn the stalk and slice the strips into threads, then slice the threads into tiny pieces.

If you DO have a hand blender, just cut the stalks into smaller ½ inch pieces and continue.

Tip:
The ONLY answer to "Do I look fat?" is not to answer, period. Offer to go shoe shopping...and live.

Put broccoli stalks into a sauce pan with ½ cup water and a little butter. Cook until the broccoli is tender, stirring occasionally. This is ONE example where the broccoli doesn't have to be cooked perfectly al dente, but it shouldn't be mush either. Add a pinch of salt, ground pepper, and garlic powder.

Once the broccoli is tender, turn off the stove, and stir in the can of cream of chicken soup and a couple tablespoonfuls of sour cream. Mix well. If you decided to use your hand blender, here is your opportunity. Put the hand blender into the bowl and push the button to pulse it a few times until the broccoli bits are soup bits. CAUTION: Be careful as you press the button; the soup may swirl up to the top and fling everywhere. Broccoli soup burns are not attractive, especially if you are cooking naked. Seriously, do NOT ever cook naked.[45] Unless you are a kitchen stud like us, and even we only cook things that don't spatter.

If you want to give the soup a little kick, grate some extra sharp cheddar cheese onto the hot soup and let it melt in. Grub.

Avgolemono Soup

Can of condensed Chicken and Rice soup
Fresh lemon juice

Butter
1 Egg

This recipe is so easy, even you probably aren't going to need to man up to get 'er done. Open the can of soup, and follow the directions on the label to make the soup, but use a slightly bigger pot. Add a pat of butter to the pot. (A pat is about the size of what you would put on your bread if you were buttering toast. The size of a pat of butter varies with the size of one's waistline. Don't hold back on our account, although your doctor may disagree...)

---

[45] Wear shoes too. Not thongs. Either kind. Trust us on this. This is, however, one of the few times it's fashionable and appropriate to wear those hideous Crocs. A la Mario Batali.

Crack the egg into a separate bowl and add a little lemon juice to it, say, one-half a small lemon. With a fork, whip the egg and lemon juice like a dominatrix with her toy. The egg and lemon juice should be smooth and properly chastised when done. Add a little soup from the pot, and whip some more until creamy smooth and completely submissive.

When the soup is simmering (don't boil over, fireboy!), add the egg-lemon mixture in and stir together. Keep stirring until the soup slightly thickens and turns a nice, white, creamy texture.[46] Remove the soup immediately from the heat to cool it down. We like to set the pan in cool water in the sink to cool it immediately. Taste the soup. It should be creamy with a slightly lemony flavor, not too strong on the lemon. If you can't taste the lemon, add a little more, and stir well.

If strings of eggs appear in the soup, you may have cooked it too long, or too hot. You can remove the egg strings using a hand blender, or simply eat them.

Baked Potatoes

Soundtrack: *Hot Potato* by Naughty by Nature

Okay nukeboy, step the hell away from that microwave. We're serious; if you even so much as think about it, close the book and return it. Okay, don't do that! We are not that proud. Well, we are, but we do not sell out on microwave potatoes. Much.

Several large Russet potatoes (or just one)	Olive oil
Himalayan pink rock salt in grinder	Sour cream or Crème Fraiche
Butter	Freshly ground pepper
Optional Accessories:	
Smoked Salmon[47]	Peppercorn sauce (recipe on page 50)
Playboy Perfect Pasta Sauce (recipe on page 70)	Caviar
Bacon pieces	Curried chicken leftovers
Grated cheese	Chives
Olives	Steamed broccoli
Cheese sauce (not that artificial crap! See page 66)	

Heat your oven to 350 degrees. Wash those potatoes thoroughly and scrub them with soap and a stiff brush in running water. Keep in mind potatoes are raised in dirt and cow shit and we need extra bull like we need more STDs.

Dry the spud, then using a regular fork, poke holes all over the spud. Do not forget to do that, or you WILL have a spud hand grenade going off in your oven and you don't want to clean up that mess. Coat lightly with olive oil by using a paper towel slightly moistened with olive oil. Sprinkle with the Himalayan salt and place potato directly on the rack in top of the oven. Put a baking sheet or some tinfoil on the lower oven rack to catch drippings.

> Step AWAY from the microwave!

Bake for one hour until the potato skin is crisp, but the potato beneath feels soft to your fork. If you're cooking more than four potatoes, cook for an extra 15 minutes. Cut the potato open - careful of the steam! It should be the BEST, both flaky and delicious.

---

[46] we assume this consistency is familiar to you, yes?

[47] Also known as "lox"

Cauliflower and Cheese Saucy Sauce

Soundtrack: *Big Cheese* by Nirvana

Simple flavors can really blow your mind. This is a very simple meal, or a great side dish. When you get it at the Farmer's market, the cauliflower should have dark green leafage still on it, and the cauliflower head itself should be very white. You will want a good Monterey Jack cheese for this, with a little Colby cheese tossed in for color and flavor. If you can get the Tarragon fresh, do so, of course.

Head of cauliflower	Tarragon
Chili powder	Cheese sauce (on page 66)

Find the vegetable steamer basket, that metal thing that looks like a radar dish from a space ship. Yeah, it is a vegetable steamer, NOT a VW parts washer. We understand your confusion.

Find a lidded pot that the steamer will fit into. Fill the bottom inch or so of the pot with water, and then set the steamer basket in there. The steamer basket holds the veggies up off the water, but allows steam to get through to cook the veggies. Get the water boiling while you are handling your cauliflower.

Break out the cauliflower and your chef's knife. Very carefully cut the tops of the cauliflower where the cauliflower branches are about a ½ to ¼-inch thick. Just like broccoli, those little cauliflower heads are called "florets" because some Frenchie thought they looked like a "little flower."

Tip:
Walk softly and carry a GINORMOUS box of chocolates.

Set the cauliflower florets into the steamer, cover, and cook for about 15 minutes. Remove the lid, and with a fork, carefully grab a piece of cauliflower and bite the stem; if it is softer than crunchy, it is done. Get the cauliflower out of the water before it turns to mush. Be careful draining the hot water from the bottom of the pot. We wouldn't want you to have that freshly boiled look.

Whip up a batch of the cheese sauce (page 66), using Jack and Colby cheeses. Season with chili powder and tarragon 'til it just about bites back. Plate and pour on the cheesy sauce. Enjoy.

Hmong Ass-Burner

Soundtrack: *Welcome to the Jungle* by Guns and Roses

In the mountainous regions of Vietnam are a group of people called the Hmong. They are known for at least two bad-ass things: killing communists, and a tasty hot salsa. Okay maybe they are not known for the salsa, but I think they should be.

A friend of ours, Brandon NeJame, got this recipe from a clan of Hmong that adopted him as their friend (and he is The Man because he sent Jim a frozen batch of this by snail mail, and then got us the recipe from a Hmong Mama when we begged for it).

Thai chile peppers (green or red)	1/4 cup of cilantro (finely chopped)
Green onion (stalk only)	1 cup lime juice
Fish sauce or Bragg's Liquid Amino Acid	Ground salt
Optional: Monosodium glutamate	

Go to your local Asian market. Don't be afraid if you're not Asian; they're cool. Select the green or red Thai chili peppers, the full size ones. Remove the stems and then use a blender (wussy method) or finely chop with your 8-inch chef's knife (manly method) until you have a ½ cup. If Thai peppers are not in season, or you don't have time

to hunt for them, you can substitute Jalapenos, or Serrano peppers, but they are second class to the real deal. Add ⅓ cup Fish sauce. Yeah, that's right, I said Fish sauce. It's fermented fish STUFF. You don't really need to know the details. All you need to know is: it's fermented (good), and it tastes good. Don't be a baby, just get it. Brandon recommended "Three Crabs" fish sauce. Pick it up at the Asian market when you're purchasing your Thai peppers.

If you can't stand the thought (or taste) of fish sauce, you can use the unfortunately named "Bragg's Liquid Aminos." Sounds like hell. Tastes pretty amazing.

A word about lime juice. The crap they sell in a plastic pseudo-citrus bottle isn't lime juice. It's lime piss. Get REAL limes and squeeze them. The two handled metal citrus squeezers (usually painted bright orange) are an acceptable method. Go get one. Slice the lime in half and place it cut fresh side down into the squeezers "bowl" with the holes, then close the handles and squeeze. Easy, no seeds. Remove lime rind. Repeat.

If you don't have the juice squeezer, cut the lime in half and squeeze it over your cupped other hand, letting the juice dribble through your fingers while catching the seeds between your fingers.

Salt to taste, as the fish sauce can vary depending on what you got. (If in doubt, add ½ tsp and add more from there to taste)

You can also add a pinch of MSG, a.k.a., Monosodium glutamate. MSG adds the "Umami" flavor, a.k.a. savoriness. Your mama knew it by the name "Accent" before the world freaked out over the stuff and thought it caused everything from hemorrhoids to headaches. In some people it actually DOES cause headaches, but it has been found to be harmless for most people (including us) by the Supergeeks that should know. Don't laugh, those Supergeeks also invented the nuclear bomb, so you will be respectful, worm.

Mix all that stuff up and put it in a bottle, or a bucket, and store it sealed in the fridge. If you're not dude enough to handle the heat, you can cool the peppers down by adding ¼ cup water, or more lime juice. You also could select a different pepper like Poblanos or Serranos, although it will change the taste.

The Hmong apparently eat this with good stuff like boiled pork. We bow low to their choice. But where we live, this is the PERFECT sauce for the most bad-ass Carne Asada Tacos north of the Ho Chi Minh Trail, or at least Tijuana.

Don't be shy; you're gonna need lots o' tacos when you taste this sauce.

Guacamole

Soundtrack: *Hot Summer Nights* by Nickelback

Grab two avocados from the Farmer's market. Since you are not yet studly enough to pick them, tell the farmer when you plan to use them and let them pick for you. While you're at the market, see if you can find some fresh sourdough bread or freshly made tortilla chips. Ask for a taste test to make sure the chips are not stale.

Don't double dip the salsa, George.

2 Avocados	Tomato	Mayonnaise or sour cream
Sweet onion	Garlic	Salt
Chips or fresh sourdough bread	Fresh ground black pepper	

There is something sensuous about guacamole. It's like the curve along a woman's back right above the hip, but below the shoulder. The only thing we can think of that's better is applying the guacamole to that spot on our woman and licking it off. We digress.

Use the knife to cut the avocado skin and flesh, all the way to the pit, and circling the avocado all the way around. Start up at the narrow end of the avocado and cut all the way around the wide end, and back up to your starting point. Set the knife on the cutting board, and using both hands, twist the avocado halves. One half will shlurp[48] off of the pit. Scoop the avocado flesh out of the side with no pit and put the avocado meat into a medium sized bowl.

For the half with the pit, set the avocado on the block. Seriously, do NOT hold it in your hand for this, numbnuts. Using the knife in a small chopping motion, whack it into the pit a little way. A single Jedi chop motion is all that is needed. Do NOT do a Luke Skychopper and try to slice through the whole pit and quarter the avocado. The pit should be stuck on the knife. Twist the knife to pop it pit out of the avocado. Wrap your delicate, baby soft hand over the BACK top half of your knife and push with your fingers to pop the seed into the compost pail.

Jim is rather testy with his knife blades. He has always been suspicious of this Ninja-cado technique as it seems to be a recipe for a dull spot on the blade. After years of making guacamole, he would rather finesse the avocado pit and preserve the knife blade, kinda like trying to remove one's manhood from a compromising location while simultaneously leaving everything intact. Jim's method is to take the avocado half and coddle it in one hand and very carefully place the knife flat against the meat of the avocado and tenderly poke the tip of the 8-inch chef's knife into the pit. Do NOT get the blade edge near your hand while doing this. Gently leverage against the avocado with the edge of the blade to pop the pit out over the compost pail or *gasp* trash can. The pit should pop right out, with minimal or no damage to the blade. Jim admits he may be a little mental on this issue. His

---

[48] A technical term. That's chef talk.

wife, the Teutonic Goddess, makes him a LOT mental by grabbing the avocado halves and squeezing them until the pit explodes out like the creature in Aliens. We digress.

Remove the avocado flesh from the de-pitted half, and repeat the process for the other avocado. Dice the tomato and add it and any juices into the bowl. Dice half a sweet onion and mix in as well. Take your garlic cloves and mash them with the flat of your knife blade (careful with that sharp edge, Kung Fu) and remove the dry skin from the cloves. Cut the garlic cloves into thin slices, and then dice the slices.

The bowl should now contain a green paste with yellow, red, and onion areas. Add salt and fresh ground black pepper, but keep the avocado flavor as the dominant one. Don't add too much salt or pepper as either can overpower the rest of the bowl. Keep in mind that if you blow your taste buds away with too much salt, you'll keep adding salt and not know it's there. Easy, tiger. The chips are salted so only a little is needed.

This mixture is good to go as it is right now. You just won't have a lot of guacamole to go around, but then again, you may not want to share. We understand. In order to make enough Guac to go around, add a small amount of mayonnaise (Thomas's method) or sour cream (Jim's method) to smooth it out and make it more dip-able. Taste it. Add a little more, or not, your call. Just don't go too far or you'll be eating green chunky mayo, and that's simply nasty. (The only thing worse is the green food-dyed Ranch Dressing a Tex-Mex joint tried to pass off as "guacamole" in Galveston, but that's a horror story for another day.)

Jim's ancient family recipe doesn't use onions in the avo-dip. He insists on finding "Onion Salt" instead of the onions and salt to flavor his guacamole. However, it is getting increasingly hard to find onion salt for some strange reason. It's only for the truly dedicated man, the Scout, willing to climb the mountain using all five of his limbs. Minced onion and Himalayan salt will get 'er done, but if you find the onion salt, say hi to the Oracle of the Mountain, for Jim.

Nachos without Artificial Implants

Soundtrack: *Dr. Feelgood* by Motley Crüe

There are lots of places that serve something they call "nachos." Usually they are paper containers of nasty-ass stale chips with canned "artificial cheese product" poured over the top. Yes, we understand that is "good" in the sense that artificial breast implants are "good," but you probably don't want to live there. To build your own real stack o' nachos, follow the path below to happy guilt-full eating ecstasy. Best if you are alone, and, of course, wash up afterwards.

Bag of Doritos (whatever flavor you prefer)	Monterey Jack cheese
Goat cheese	Flagship cheese
Sausage (cooked)	Half an avocado
Black pepper	Paprika
Salsa, pick a winner (your favorite)	Black olives

Kick the oven dial onto "broiler." Pull out a cookie sheet (big flat pan), lay a sheet of foil on it, and butter the foil. Very gently lay down a layer of Doritos and sprinkle some shredded jack cheese over them. Chop up the sausage and sprinkle it all over the chips and cheese. Add a spoon or knife-full of goat cheese here and there. Spice it all with black pepper and paprika, then sprinkle the shredded Flagship cheese over the very top. Slide that into the broiler till the layers of cheese have melted. Don't burn your fingers.

Optionally, you can add salsa or hot sauce, and black olives. Chunk up the avocado and toss it on the pile. Devour.

Shit on a Shingle (SOS)

Soundtrack: *In the Navy* **by the Village People**

Yes, that *is* the official name. Would we lie to you? Much? Ask any military man. You may want to call it "Chipped Beef on Toast" to your lady friend. Or just "SOS" and change the subject. Quickly.

1 Pound full-fat burger (NOT lean - blech!)	1 Medium onion
Whole milk	Butter
White flour	Himalayan pink salt
Bay leaf	Bread (white or sourdough)

Put two slices of bread into the toaster. Throw the ground cow into a frying pan sufficiently large to hold it. Cook the burger on medium to high heat, stirring and flipping and breaking the burger up from chunks into bits, regularly. Cook until all the little burger bits are a nice brown color, but still soft when touched with a fork. Drain the oil or fat out of the pan into a bowl. Remove the burger bits to another bowl. Do NOT put the fatty oil in the sink or it will clog your pipes.[49] Yes, we like our pipes cleaned regularly too.

Remove the first pair of toast, and lock and load two more slices into the toaster. Place two tablespoons of butter into the frying pan, heat until melted, and then add one tablespoon of white flour. Mix well together until it forms a nice fluid paste like that crap glue your teacher made you use when you were a little punk.[50] The paste is called "roux,"[51] and is cool if you are a Cajun, but not cool if you are French. We kid the French (because we can).

> **Tip:**
> If you are winning the argument with her, apologize immediately.

When the roux has formed, and before it burns,[52] add a cup of milk and stir vigorously into the roux in the pan with a wooden spoon. Do NOT use a metal fork in your non-stick pan! Stir rapidly until it forms...get ready for it...gravy! Remove the gravy from heat and mix in a little salt and ground pepper.

---

[49] Fiber helps.
[50] ...and probably ate...
[51] Pronounced "roo".
[52] Always watch your heat, fire-man.

Yes, grunion, you have made white gravy. It is also known as "white sauce" or "Béchamel sauce" by the French. Don't let an Italian catch you calling it that, though. The Italians call it "Besciamella," and you don't want to get caught in the "the French stole Italian cuisine" food fight.

When white sauce is mixed with various cheeses such as cheddar, Swiss, or any other grated hard cheese it is just, well, sex. On almost any kind of food. We digress.

If you did not listen to us, and you burned the Béchamel, you now have brown gravy. TADA! It's still damn good, so don't get your knickers in a knot.

Take your hamburger and return it to the pan with whatever gravy you got. Just make sure there are no lumps in the gravy before you add the burger. Stir the gravy and burger together well. Taste with spoon. Salt and pepper as needed. Taste again, but only after you wash the spoon, cretin. Is it good? Excellent. Put a piece of toast on a plate and pour the burger sauce over it.

Congratulations, lad; you have Shit on a Shingle. Known to military men the world over, loathed by some and craved by others. We're with the others.

Soundtrack: *Green Eggs and Ham* by Big Royal and the Revue

2 or 3 large eggs	Olive oil or butter
Ground Himalayan pink salt	Ground black pepper

This recipe is going to be the basis for many more coming up, so we might as well start your eggs edumacation with basic Eggs Over-Easy. No, you are NOT allowed to make scrambled eggs. Scrambled eggs have their place, but even if you've done them before, scrambled eggs might be a challenge to your self-esteem. Why? Did you add milk and cheese and manly seasonings to your scrambled eggs? Uh huh.

Start by reading the section on cracking eggs (on page 9), or better still, you can begin by watching the video on www.manmeetstove.com/videoz and click on the "Knife Skillz" video. Pour a little olive oil in the pan and swirl it around so the pan has a very thin of coat of oil. Turn the heat down to medium low. Crack two eggs and open them close to the pan surface so they gently land in the pan without breaking the yolks. Grind some salt and pepper onto the eggs (don't overdo it!). Let the eggs cook until the bottom egg white is cooked but the top of the white is still a bit jelly-ish.[53]

Tip:
Store your chef's knife and cutting board within easy reach.

Get a thin plastic spatula and place it in the pan, flat against the bottom. While holding the pan handle with one hand and the spatula with the other, tilt the pan and quickly slide the spatula under the egg, but leave some egg hanging off the spatula end. Use the bit of egg hanging off the spatula to anchor the egg to the pan, while you gently slide the rest of the egg back in, flipping it over and trying not to break the yolk. If you're as good at sex as you claim, you should get this right the first time. Oh sorry, that's another topic.

Don't sweat it if you break the yolk, that's the egg that'll be yours. Your lady gets the good stuff.

Try again with the second egg. Once flipped, the eggs need to cook for another minute or less. Remove eggs using the quick slide-of-the-spatula trick, flipping the egg back right side up onto the plate. Put the first dynamic duo of eggs onto a plate. Do another batch of two eggs for her, and get it right this time. The whites should be cooked and the yolks should be very slightly cooked. Runny, but not fried through. This is called "Eggs Over Easy." We've known a few (over) easy in our time.

You can also cook the egg without flipping it, but pay close attention that the yolk is not fried through to be a simple fried egg. This is called "Sunny Side Up" if you must be so perky at this hour in the morning. You just got laid. We understand.

---

[53] It is TOO a word

The Morning-After Chilaquiles

Soundtrack: *Whenever, Wherever* by Shakira

Olive oil	Stale nacho cheese-flavored Doritos (or other tortilla chips)
Mild salsa or enchilada sauce	Crema Mexicana or Crème Fraiche (or sour cream if you must)
Queso Fresco (Mexican fresh cheese)	Guacamole (see page 25)
Black olives (canned or better)	2 Eggs per person

Slide out of bed so you don't wake that fine female you finally managed to finesse into spending the night with you. Put that woodie away, Tiny, and dig through the wreckage of your room. Find a bag of tortilla chips, (and in this one and only case), the staler the better. Bust out the frying pan.

First read the section on cracking eggs on page 9, then the Eggscellent recipe on page 29. When you have at least two decent over-easy eggs per person ready to go, read on.

Pour a small amount of olive oil in the pan, and drop the chips in to warm them up. Make sure they are slightly coated in the oil. Next, pour enough salsa in the pan to minimally coat the chips in salsa, then pour in just a little more. Turn the whole mess in the pan with a wooden spoon, over and over, until the chips have a good coating of salsa. When the chips are coated and have been in for a few minutes to warm up, you have Chilaquiles. Remove from the pan and plate beside the eggs. Sprinkle broken up Queso Fresco cheese on the chilaquiles.

Clear the beer cans and panties off the table, set the plates and silverware, and set sides of the Crema Mexicana, crème fraiche or sour cream, in addition to guacamole (see page 25), olives, and slices of Queso Fresco in little bowls. Each bowl should have its own spoon.

If you are out of salsa, you can use enchilada sauce, or if you're really good, you could try spaghetti sauce. But only in a pinch.

If you only have paper plates, go out and buy some plates and silverware for balls' sake. If your beer budget has exceeded your credit card, well...well done. Try a thrift store.

Breakfast Scramble

Soundtrack: *Egg Man* by the Beastie Boys

3 eggs	Olive oil	Milk
Gouda cheese (shredded)	Ground Himalayan pink salt	Fresh ground pepper
Paprika	English muffin	Grey French Dijon mustard
Avocado	Fresh fruit (cubed)	

It doesn't get any simpler than this. First, go to www.manmeetsstove.com/videoz and watch the video "Cracking Eggz." Now is the time to practice egg cracking skills.

Bust out a frying pan; that's the one that's about 12-inches across and 4 inches deep. Don't use too small a pan, or you will fill it up with ingredients while you cook, and that'll be a mess.

Throw in a little olive oil to lubricate. No, not YOU, lubricate the pan. It keeps the eggs from sticking. And, NO, don't try olive oil with your trouser-eggs either. We recommend Bacon Lube for that.

Crack the eggs into a bowl. Whip the eggs with a fork till they are evenly mixed. Add just a touch of milk and a handful of shredded Gouda cheese. Grind in some pepper, add some salt, and toss in a pinch of paprika. Turn on the stove fire to "high." See how high that fire is? That's the "I'm gonna burn this to black and stink up the house with egg smoke" flame height. NO. Turn the heat down to medium, or even low. Put the pan on the fire, and pour the egg-cheese mixture in the pan. If you have a non-stick Teflon pan, DO NOT USE METAL UTENSILS IN THE PAN. Capiche? Grab a wooden spoon and stir the eggs. This is known as "scrambling" them. You don't have to continuously stir, but it won't hurt, and might keep you from overcooking or burning the scramble.

When all of the liquid is out of the eggs and they have turned white, you're done. If you like your eggs on the moist-side,[54] you can pull the scramble off the burner with a little liquid remaining. That's good grub too.

Grab an English muffin and split it in half with a fork. Toast the English muffin halves, then skim one slice with butter and the other with Dijon Mustard (not too much!). Thinly slice some avocado, put it on the muffin with some of the egg scramble, and close the two muffin halves up to make a sandwich. When it's time to eat, put some fruit on the plate, but only eat the fruit if observed by a spousal unit.[55]

Jim's Spicy Rice with Eggs

Soundtrack: *The Spicy McHaggis Jig* by Dropkick Murphys

Pepper-infused spicy olive oil	Basmati rice	Rice vinegar
Salt	2 eggs per person	

This is standard Sunday fare for Jim and his Lusty Lass. Bust out the rice cooker we told you to buy. Put a cup of rice, a cup and half of water, and a pinch of salt into the rice cooker and press the button. If you want more rice, double the recipe. If you want the rice moister (and who doesn't want that?) add another half cup of water per cup of rice.

Basmati is our preferred rice of choice, but any non-instant rice will do. Forget the candy-ass box o' rice. Real Men™ buy rice in 10 or 20 pound bags and hump that sucker to their monster truck. Rice is relatively cheap and easy grub; once you use it and see how easy and good it is…we think you'll use it a lot more.

After the rice cooker is done, bust out a big frying pan. Throw some spicy olive oil into the bottom of the pan (as much heat as you can take) and some regular olive oil. If you can't find the spicy olive oil, you can add some hot pepper sauce like rooster sauce, instead. When the oil is warmed up a bit (but not smoking), throw the cooked rice into the pan, and let it fry for a little bit. You want it to fry till you get some browning on the bottom, but not too much. You can check the browning by lifting the edge of the rice up with a spoon or spatula. Stir the rice and let it brown a little more on the bottom. Throw in a bit of rice vinegar. If you notice it drying out before this, feel free to throw in some rice vinegar then. Taste. If it's tasty grub, plate it. Cook up some of the Eggsellent Eggs from page 29 (two per person). When the eggs are done, place them over the rice.

---

[54] …and who doesn't?
[55] This is known as "misdirection." Getting caught using misdirection is called "blue balls."

Barry's Waffle

Soundtrack: Copacabana by Barry Manilow
(We kid. Don't listen to that or your brain will ooze out of your ears.)
Actual Soundtrack: California Gurls by Katy Perry

SPECIAL EQUIPMENT REQUIRED: Waffle Maker

Box or bag of waffle mix	Seltzer water (if required by the box instructions)
Butter	Peanut butter
Fresh berries, as many kinds as you can find	Cream and/or vanilla yogurt

The waffle is really the perfect breakfast-in-bed food. It's not too crumbly. It's just one thing, so it is easy to keep on the plate, and the waffle maker makes them one at a time anyway. So, the only drawback is that you have to get up, you slovenly sod.

Dig out the waffle maker. We have had great performance from a Toastmaster Belgian waffle maker over 14 years old, but buy whatever you like. Pick your poison for waffle mixes; just be aware that if you get one that needs seltzer water, then make sure you pick up the seltzer water. No one wants to see you at the butt-crack-of-dawn on Sunday morning roaming the halls of the local stop-n-rob market looking for a one serving bottle of seltzer. If you do need to go out, don't forget your pants. No one wants to see that, either.

Follow the directions on the box, mostly, but use melted butter instead of the oil they call for and shake cinnamon into the batter as you stir. Don't overfill the waffle maker. Less is more when you first are trying to figure it out. Kinda like when you first tried to French-kiss a girl and you thought it was all about tongues. What she felt was you using your tongue like an impaling sword. Bad. Gentle, and always leave her wanting more, is a good rule of thumb. Thumbs we'll talk about later.[56]

Wash two handfuls of your berries and set them in a medium glass bowl.[57] Take the tops off of any berries with stems. Toss some sugar in. Fork the berries. No, don't go all American Pie on us....we mean use a fork to mash the berries up a bit and to stir the sugar in. Have a plate, fork, knife, and napkin ready to go. When the waffle maker speaks to your inner-one-true-self and tells you that the waffle is done,[58] carefully use a fork to get the waffle out of the maker (don't scratch a non-stick surface!!!) and plate the waffle. Apply generous amounts of butter and peanut butter to the waffle. Now use a ladle to cover the waffle with your berries. Pour some cream or spoon yogurt on top of your berries, then serve.

Great. Now we can't get that image from American Pie out of our heads. Thanks.

---

[56] Or maybe we shouldn't.
[57] If your berries are a handful, we hope for your sake, that she has big hands.
[58] No, numbnuts, a light on the waffle maker will go on, or off, or a bell will ding.

Pancakes

Soundtrack: *Buttons* by the Pussycat Dolls

If you've gotten this far, we think you're ready to make a pancake, flapjack, Johnnycake, griddlecake, or as we prefer to call them, a butter-n-maple syrup delivery system. We like 'em thin and crispy. Like a sunburned supermodel. Actually, we don't like that, but we thought it was funny. Pancakes are believed to be one of the earliest forms of foods created on earth. This is why you need to eat them early in the morning.[59]

Box or bag of pancake mix	Peanut butter
Milk	Butter
Honey	Heavy cream
Oil	Real maple syrup

Grab what ever box-o-pancake mix you prefer and mix up a batch according to the instructions on the box. Once you have a bowl full of battery goo, check the consistency; it should be closer to motor oil than to toothpaste in texture. Get the skillet heated up over a medium flame. Use as light-tasting of a vegetable oil as you have, preferably canola oil, and pour in just enough to barely cover the bottom of the pan with a thin film of oil. Grab a ladle (small bowl-like spoon) and use it to scoop up some batter. Pour a roughly 5-inch ring of batter and then slowly spiral inward till you close the center. Let it fry, but watch for bubbles to form in the batter. When some of the bubbles have started to pop, flip the flapjack over with a spatula. The underside should be brown and crispy looking with some crispy "edges" that follow that spiral inward. When the underside is toast brown, plate that bad boy. You're done, Jack.

If you are really into stacked – and aren't we all – start with four pancakes. On the bottom pancake, spread peanut butter, place the next pancake on the first, spread butter on this one, stack up the next one, and apply more of the peanut butter. Repeat to get a stack of four. Now drizzle honey or maple syrup all over the stack, and pour a bit of heavy cream on for kicks. If you use this creative idea somewhere else, we recommend the acquisition of some plastic sheets first, and avoid getting the honey into any crevice-type places...[60]

Eggz Benedict

Soundtrack: *Love is a Battlefield* by Pat Benatar

2 English muffins	2 Eggs	Ham
Avocado	Large tomato	Hollandaise sauce (page 67)

So if you have a really special occasion and you fully intend to excite her taste buds and get her naughty bits all tingly, this may be the dish for you. But it is going to take some preparation, so distract her by giving her the TV remote control[61] or other battery operated device. Head over to page 67 and whip up some hollandaise. That sound you hear is our evil laugh at your attempts to perfect hollandaise. Hang in there, dude, it's REALLY worth it.

Once your hollandaise is done, grab an English muffin and, using a fork, stab into the side of the muffin about mid-way, repeatedly, then press your thumb into the side of the muffin you just forked, gently! Think of it as a lesson you will hopefully have use for later. A gentle thumb works best. The muffin should split pretty cleanly into two halves. Put the muffin halves into the toaster, ready to go once the eggs are almost done.

Now, prepare a couple of eggs following the instructions in Eggsellent Eggs (page 29). While the eggs are cooking, slice the tomato into ¼-inch slices or so. Throw away the end slices. You just need the two best slices from the

---

[59] No, not really
[60] Trust us.
[61] No, really. You can do this. Once.

middle that are about the size of your English muffin halves. Set the muffins to toasting, and ready two plates. When the muffins pop up, grab them and place them open-face on the plate.

Use your knife to cut the avocado skin and flesh, all the way to the pit, and circling the avocado all the way around the long way. Start up at the top at the narrow end of the avocado and cut all the way back to your starting point. Set the knife on the cutting board and, using both hands, twist the avocado halves. One half will schlurp[62] off of the pit. Scoop the avocado flesh out of the side with no pit and put the avocado meat into a medium bowl.

For the half with the pit, set the avocado on the block (wrap a towel – not your hand! – around it to hold it in place if you need to), and use the knife in a chopping motion whack it into the pit a little way. A single Jedi chop motion is all that is needed. Do NOT do a Samurai Whack and slice through the whole pit and quarter the avocado. The pit should now be stuck on the knife. Twist to remove, and pop the seed into the compost pail.

Jim is rather testy with his knife blades.[63] He has always been suspicious of this Ninja-cado technique as it seems to be a recipe for a dull spot on the blade. After years of making guacamole, he would rather finesse the avocado pit and preserve the knife blade. Take the avocado half and coddle it in one hand[64] and very carefully poke the tip of the 8-inch chef's knife into the pit next to the meat of the avocado. Do NOT get the blade edge near your hand while doing this. Now, gently leverage against the avocado with the edge of the blade to pop the pit out over the compost pail or *gasp* trash can. The pit should pop right out, with minimal or no damage to the blade. Jim admits he may be a little mental on this issue.

To remove the flesh from the avocado halves, take the avocado half and coddle it in your hand. With the other hand, get a butter knife and gently slice from the pointy end of the avocado to the round end, following the interior skin of the avocado with the tip of the knife. Move over a ¼-inch and slice again, parallel to the first cut, and repeat. Now take a tablespoon (the big one) and carefully scoop the avocado slices out with the spoon, again by following the interior skin of the avocado with the spoon to remove each slice.

Lay down a delicious slice of ham on one half of your English muffin, and then a few of the avocado slices to cover the ham. Pour a healthy dose of Hollandaise over ham and avocado. Pour more Hollandaise sauce on the second muffin half and place a slice of heirloom tomato on top. Sprinkle with freshly ground salt and pepper. When we say a "healthy" amount of Hollandaise, you should FEEL your arteries clogging up as you pour. Repeat with the other half muffin. When you have a heart attack, you're done.[65]

The dish is meant to be eaten as an open-face sandwich, with a knife and fork. However, if you can squeeze all that Hollandaise onto the halves, make it into a sandwich, then eat it without looking like a slob? We applaud you.

---

[62] What? Of COURSE it's a real word! You don't think we make this crap up, do you?

[63] He also gets nervous with knives near his testes, quite a coincidence…

[64] Insert your own punch line here

[65] This is a joke. Do not attempt to eat this much Hollandaise at home. We are trained professionals.

stuffing buns (sandwiches)

Ode to the Sandwich

What could be better than to place your lips on luscious buns
delectable morsels of cheese, cold cuts and Mayo
Spread to the edges
Egg-salad and Dijon Mustard
Hidden between
the cold cuts lie treasures indeed
chopped onion and a little button green olive
slices of hardboiled egg
Bits of Bacon and slices of cucumber

Oh the Sandwich, how do I love thee, let me count the ways

- Thomas Jacques

We have to talk. There are things your mother never told you, and your Dad just didn't know. That thing you do in the kitchen with the 94¢ loaf of white bread, store brand mustard, and the plastic wrapped "processed cheese food product" is not a sandwich. Your mom should have told you. She probably was too busy keeping you from killing yourself with your Real Chemistry Set.™ Our moms sure were.

The following are the Six Commandments[66] of sandwich-building.

Bread – Your bread should be selected from a local bakery, not a corporation. The kind of bread you're looking for was baked this morning and they probably had to slice it for you. You spend 7 bucks on a processed meal at the "fast food" place down the road and it: 1) sucks and 2) sort-of-feeds-you for a meal. A good loaf might set you back four Washingtons and will be the foundation for 6 to 8 Fantastiwiches. So get good bread. And it wouldn't hurt if you had a few good grains or seeds or nuts in the thing.[67]

Quality Condiments – Condiments are the various liquid/paste things you add to the sandwich, such as mustard, ketchup, hot sauce, salsa, and caviar.[68] The moisture and much of the flavor comes from these. Buy great tasting condiments in small jars until you learn what you like, use, and more importantly, how much to use. It's better to use up the small jar of gray mustard than to end up using the 5 gallon jug of mayonnaise long after its "use me by" date.[69]

Condiment location – Sandwiches are an amalgam,[70] or union of textures and flavors. Each bite should get an equal share, so mayonnaise, jam, and/or some form of nut-butter (like peanut butter) is spread to the edge of each slice. If you are trying to save up your fats for a rainy day, then spread a thinner layer, but always cover the bread slice. Mustard, catsup, relish, horseradish and other flavor heavy-hitters do not need to be continuous, but they need to be evenly placed across the bread slice.

Meat & Cheese – Thick or thin, triangles or squares, meats and cheeses will come in every shape and size. Your goal is to make layers that spread the lovin' across the loaf. We understand if the sandwich weighs four pounds after this layer.

Veggies – The added texture and moisture are the main reasons these are in sandwiches. Oh, and someone told us they are good for us.[71]

Spices – In a sandwich? Frack yeah! Even a crap cook salts his eggs while he burns them. The vegetables and meats need spices. Sometimes the flavor comes from the condiments, but sometimes you need to toss a pinch of oregano up into the air over your meatloaf sandwich, or flutter[72] some sage onto your chicken breasts and cheese on rye. So don't ask...do. If you don't know what you like, then toss something in there and see if you like it. You know, the same method you use in your sex life.

---

[66] Moses was an over-achiever. Who needs 10 Commandments?

[67] Jim objects to this on ethical grounds. Grains are feed for cows to be later eaten as steak.

[68] Okay, maybe only Jim uses this as a condiment.

[69] Seriously, expiration dates matter. Like a great steakhouse, don't go past them.

[70] Amalgam is Thomas's pretentious word for "mixture." "Pretentious" is Jim's snobbish word for "snobby."

[71] A government conspiracy.

[72] Yeah, Thomas used flutter there. I couldn't touch that.

Grilled Cheese Sandwich Three-Way

Moron-Simple Grilled Cheese

Soundtrack: *Unskinny Bop* by Poison

Start here, it's fast and easy. Like a quickie. Get some!

White or sourdough bread Butter	Firm cheese, like cheddar, Swiss, or Jack

Slice the cheese as thin as you reasonably can. You'll want enough cheese to fill the sandwich edge to edge. Butter two bread slices on both sides, top and bottom. That's right, butter the OUTSIDE too. If butter is not all over your monkey-stumps and the cutting board, you're doing it wrong. Place the cheese you sliced before you got your hands covered in butter and lay them on one piece of bread, then slap the other slice of bread on top. What? You didn't slice the cheese first? Dude.

Break out the frying pan, fire it up on medium heat, and set the bread, butter, and cheese assembly in the pan. It should sizzle like a high school cheerleader. When the cheese starts to melt and the bread smells like toast, flip it over. It should be golden brown on the top. If it's black, you either cooked it too long, or too hot. After turning, again wait for the toast smell and pull it out. Yeah, I said it. Dig in.

If you've got that sandwich down, welcome to the party, you now can cook like a five year-old.

Take it up a notch. Let's rumble.

Almost-Got–a-Pair Grilled Cheese

Soundtrack: *Velcro Fly* by ZZ Top

You can use this one for a date in a pinch, but you better have a good excuse, like the burned carcass of whatever you are claiming you were *going* to prepare.

Bread (white, sourdough, French, or potato bread) Monterey Jack cheese Black pepper	Cheddar cheese Paprika Butter

Slice the cheese thin, and slice enough cheese to cover the bread from edge to edge. Cut some butter off the block (yes, butter comes in a block, get over it) and warm it in the microwave in a bowl. Yes, we just told you to use a microwave. Yes, you should feel dirty like a church boy with porn. Actually, using the nuke for melting and SOME tasks is okay, but don't overcook it! Stand there and watch till it's melted. If you must, think about Britney Spears, Pamela Anderson, or Marilyn Monroe[73] while you wait. On second thought, don't think about that; you'll lose focus and burn the butter. Now, grind some black pepper into the butter bowl, spoon in the paprika, and stir. Now you have flavored butter, congratulations. Useful stuff. Tasty. Chill the butter and then butter the two bread slices, both sides. Place both kinds of cheese on one buttered slice, and slap the other bread slice on top.

Grab the frying pan, set it on medium heat, and place the bread, butter, and cheese construct in the pan. It should sizzle. You know from the first grilled cheese recipe when to flip it over. After turning, wait for the toast smell and slide it out of the pan. If you can slide it out of the pan, right onto the plate, you're almost good. Serve to your saucy wench.

---

[73] How old ARE you anyway?

Grilled Cheese with Balls

Soundtrack: *Bark at the Moon* by Ozzy Osbourne

Now for the serious Grilled Cheese, this is one of those I'm-stuck-at-a-cousin's-house-with-no-porn-and-they-are-all-gone-for-the-day-so-what-do-I-eat dishes.

GOOD sourdough bread	Extra sharp cheddar
Goat cheese with herbs	Block of parmesan
Butter	Good olives (we like Kalamata)

Good olives come with a pit (the rock-like seed in the center), and there are three ways to get the pit out.

Method 1: Grab the olive and simply squeeze the seed out with your fingers, leaving the meat of the olive in between your fingers. This will work for some soft olives, not for others. [Warning: do NOT try this with nipples, she'll smack you stupid. Unless she likes to play rough, in which case, bully for you.]

Method 2: Next, try placing the olive on your cutting board, holding onto the handle of the knife with one hand, then set your giant, badass, 8-inch chef's knife on the olive, flat to the board, and carefully push down on the flat of the blade with your free hand. I don't even WANT to know what you are doing with that other hand, but it better be holding the handle of the knife. Do NOT put your pressing hand near the edge of the blade. Ever. The flat of the blade should crush the olive and allow you to remove the pit.

Method 3: Lastly, get a small paring knife. The paring knife is the small one with a pocket knife-sized blade. NO, don't use your nasty-ass pocket knife…we KNOW where that's been. Take the paring knife and carefully cut the skin of the olive all the way around and then remove the pit with your fingers. Try not to cut the pit, as it will dull your blade faster than a groupie on a rockstar with coke.

After you have removed the pits, chop the meat of the olives into small bits, and mix into the goat cheese and set aside. Grate some parmesan. Toast the bread in the toaster. Butter the hot toast; don't hold back now! Spread the olive goat cheese, stack the cheddar on both open faces, and slap it together. Smear some extra butter on the outside, and finally sprinkle that with the parmesan (you may have to pat it into the butter to make it stick). Fry it golden brown, as described before. You won't be sorry.

Variations on the theme: You can mix up cheeses and olives; just keep the soft cheese, firm cheese, and dry cheese trifecta going.

X-Rated Grilled Cheese

Soundtrack: *De Do Do Do, De Da Da Da* by the Police

Okay, we lied, there are actually four grilled cheese sandwiches. Good things come in threes. Great things come with excess.   Here is what you are going to need.

Tomatoes	Gruyere cheese
Fresh basil	Fresh thyme
Sourdough bread	

Prepare the bread with butter like you did before, getting it everywhere fun. Put the Gruyere on a slice at a time. Pile on the tomatoes and basil and thyme to form layers of cheesy tomato goodness. Close the sandwich up and get ready to grill.

Clean the grill. We know that this has probably never occurred to you before, but the fire is not actually a perfect cleaning agent. Preheat the cleaned grill and then turn it down to low. Brush oil onto the grill grating and carefully set the sandwiches on the grill. Keep an eye on them; if they burst into flame then you had the grill up too high. Use tongs or a spatula to lift the top bread slice occasionally to check the cheese. When it starts to melt in the center, then flip it over.

Pull the smoky slabs of cheesy deliciousness off the grill and plate them; serve with a cold adult beverage, or with a cold adult. These ought to heat you both up.

Tomato Open-Face Sandwich

Soundtrack: *I Believe* by Tears for Fears

When we are old farts living in the *Blade Runner* future, few memories of summer will be as fresh as picking a tomato, slicing it up, and eating it on an open-face sandwich before the tomato loses the sun's warmth. That, and memories of Jenna Jameson.

Sourdough bread	Mayonnaise
Heirloom beefsteak tomato	Paper-thin slice of sweet onion (Walla Walla preferred)
Pinch of basil leaves (from the backyard)	Salt and cracked pepper

Grab a couple of slices of sourdough and start the bread toasting; don't stop to ponder where the toast comes from and where the bread goes, that is not for you to decide. Set out the mayonnaise, spices, and the tomato knife. Don't even say you don't have a tomato knife. It's a knife that has serrations, not a flat edge. You can use a steak knife if you must. Head out to the backyard and pick a big ripe tomato, or if you must, get an Heirloom tomato from your local grocer or Farmer's market. Give the tomato a quick wash. De-stem it with the point of the knife, slice it, and grab the toast. Mayonnaise your toast all the way to the edge and lay on the onion slices. Stack the tomato on top and apply the love with the spices.

A word about cutting onions and not crying like a little boy. There are a number of ways to avoid the onions causing you tears: A) Chill the onions before you cut them. B) Use a sharp knife. Duh, right? It actually helps, plus we already told you to keep your knife sharp, dude. C) Breathe through your mouth, not your nose, while cutting the onions. Alternatively, you can stick your tongue out while you cut the onion. This apparently helps, and makes us laugh thinking about you doing it. D) Lastly, try cutting the onion under water.   Yeah, we don't like this method either.

Instead of all that, go to www.manmeetsstove.com/videoz and click on the "Knife Skillz" video we have lovingly prepared for you, worm.

You can change it up by adding cheese or avocado to the sandwich, or make it richer by sprinkling a little Balsamic vinegar on the tomatoes.   If you want to be a stud, let's make a Balsamic Reduction.

Balsamic Reduction

Soundtrack: *Candyman* by Christina Aguilera

Bust out a bottle of balsamic vinegar, pour into a small pot, and turn on the heat. Note the line of the pan where the balsamic is. When the balsamic starts to boil, let it continue until half of it is gone (based on the original pan-line where you started). Do NOT go past the half way mark, burn dog. If you want to kick it up a notch, add minced garlic before you start the reduction. The Balsamic Reduction should be like syrup when it's done. Taste it. Yeah, that's right. If you happen to have a grilled steak, hit it with that.

Peanut Butter and Banana

Sound Track: *My Dick* by Mickey Avalon

Bananas	Nutella
White bread	Butter (NOT margarine)
Creamy peanut butter	Marshmallow cream (yeah, the white "fluff")

So you may be thinking to yourself, peanut butter and banana sandwiches? Really? If you thought that because you already eat them, excellent; quit bitchin' and move on. If you think they are beneath you, it makes us wonder what you actually have hanging beneath you…

Get some bread; any white rustic bread will work fine, and toast it. While still hot, apply butter (yeah, butter) to both slices generously, and go all the way to the edge. Don't wimp out now; do it right! Apply the peanut butter (the real stuff with sugar) and again, go all the way to the edges, but only on one piece of toast. Slice a just-ripe banana length-wise, and lay the slices down on the peanut butter. Spread a little marshmallow cream on the banana (bring on the fluff!) and spread Nutella on the other slice and be generous (to the edges, duh!), and put the slices together. Now here's the tricky part; butter the top and bottom (outside) of the sandwich, and set into an already medium hot frying pan, and fry it till slightly golden brown (the grilled cheese sandwich treatment, see below).

Do NOT burn the outsides of the sandwich. Now you have something to help address those unaddressed feelings of abandonment as a child.[74] Kidding!

Peanut Butter and Pickle Sandwich

Sound Track: Again, *My Dick* by Mickey Avalon

Yes, you did read that right. Yeah, some of us were skeptical, too (Jim), but Thomas always craves this one, despite not being preggers.   Try it.

Multigrain bread	Butter (NOT margarine)
Peanut butter	Extra spicy "Bread and Butter" pickles

Take two pieces of multi-grain bread, and spread butter, then peanut butter on each slice. Cover with a layer of overlapping extra-spicy bread-n-butter pickles. Take the delicacy that you have just prepared and go stand on the back deck of Gramma's place and eat, holding the sandwich out over the deck (pickle juice drips). Or, embrace your inner-redneck and let the drips run down your shirt. We understand.

---

[74] See a therapist for balls' sake.

Egg Salad with Sun-Dried Tomato Sandwich

Soundtrack: *New Sensation* by INXS

We say if you make this and feed it to her, you should be able to talk her out of her panties as smoothly as James Bond. We know we have.

You're gonna need six hard-boiled eggs, if you are cooking for two. If it's for one, well, you're gonna have to find someone to share it with, so get to chasing skirt. Or pants, if that's how you roll. If you're cooking for three, then what are you reading our book for? What a show-off.

To create perfect hard-boiled eggs, carefully place the eggs into a pot and add water until the eggs are covered about an inch. Put the pot on the stove and turn heat all the way up. Keep an eye on the eggs and when the water starts boiling, turn off the heat and remove the pot from the burner. Let the eggs sit for 10 minutes in the hot water. After 10 minutes, place the pot in the sink and run cold water into the pot until all the water and eggs are cool/cold. To peel the eggs, set an egg onto a hard surface and gently crack it on its side (not the ends), then roll the egg. If done properly, the middle of the shell cracks, while the ends don't, making it easier to peel off.

Bread (sourdough or crusty white bread recommended)	6 hard-boiled eggs
Mayonnaise	Sun-dried tomatoes
Ground salt and pepper	Baby lettuce greens

Pop two pieces of bread into the toaster and head over to the cutting board with your boiled eggs. To remove the eggshells, roll the eggs on the cutting board with the flat of your hand to break the shells, peel them, and discard the shells. Place into a bowl that will hold all of the eggs, add 1 to 2 tablespoons of mayo, and grind some salt and pepper on top. Mix the mayo into the eggs, breaking the eggs up as you go. Try to leave the eggs a little chunky (bite size). If you overwork them into a paste, well, that's okay, but it just doesn't look as tasty. After mixing, taste the egg/mayo mixture and add a little salt, as necessary.

Take a few of the sundried tomatoes out of the bottle, shake off the excess oil, and place them on a little plate or saucer. With a fork, squish the sundried tomatoes on the saucer into something like a paste. When the toast pops out, spread the sundried tomato paste onto the bread. It should just be a thin layer. Now, add a few baby greens, just enough to cover the bread with one layer. Pile the egg salad on over the greens. No, REALLY pile it on. You want it a little close to falling off the bread like water flows off Daisy Duke's shirt. No, we don't know what that means either, but we like thinking about Daisy Duke's wet shirt. For the adventurous, a little mustard to taste may be worth adding, provided it isn't that nasty yellow (pseudo-French) stuff.

meat

There is only one real kind of meat, and it ain't white like chicken. It's red like beef, or pink like pork. When the recent health craze kicked in, Americans decided that fat on a steak or pork was a bad thing. What crazy asshat decided a pig should be SKINNY, much less a cow? Still, that is what happened.

Perhaps you have heard of a really tasty Japanese beef called "Kobe Beef." You know why it's so tasty? Because the Japanese don't have room to grow beef like Americans do, so they want it to be PERFECT. To be FATTY. They grow their cattle special and make sure the cows are really fat bastards. Yummm. So, when you go to the market, do not look for "extra lean," red-only meat. You are looking for "marbled" meat that is red with lots of white streaks running through it.

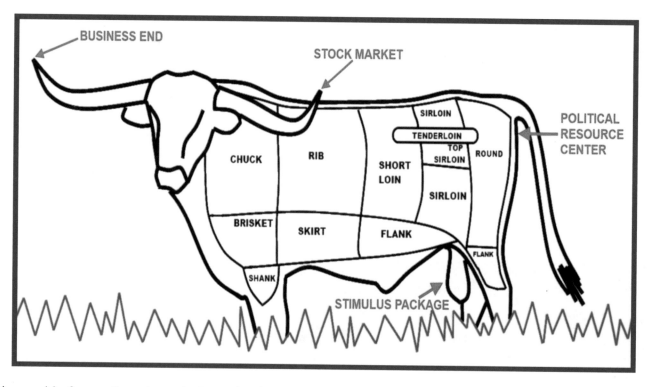

In the world of cow, there is a whole study of steaks and various cuts of beef. As we all know, the best cuts of meat are the best pieces of ass. Not the ass itself, mind you, but, you know, *around* the ass.

- **Filet Mignon/Tenderloin** – Top steak. People do eat it raw. Seriously. Top price too. Filet minion is seriously lean, so it needs you to add fat to it. Bacon is always a good option, but you can also use oil, or one of the French sauces (Béarnaise, Hollandaise)
- **Ribeye** – More fatty than Filet Mignon, but less tender; also high-priced.
- **Strip Steak** – Good steak, high price.
- **Top Sirloin** – If you're looking for good meat at a good price, this is your cow.
- **Porterhouse** – Reasonable price, with the bone, but more meat than T-bone. Tasty.
- **T-bone** - Cheaper, has a bone, less meat than Porterhouse. Tasty.
- **Chuck, Round, and Flank steak** – Cheap. Tough. Bring your meat hammer.

London Broil is not a steak. It's a top round roast. Jim has been known to buy it cheap, cut it in half to make more steaks, and grill the sucker. Be sure to marinade, regardless. It's tough.

If you can afford to get grass-fed or grain-fed "free range" beef that was allowed to personally service 20 cows twice a day for his entire life, all the better. A happy cow is a tasty cow.

There is really only one way to cook a steak to its maximal steak-y goodness, and that's rare to medium. Medium only if you must. To get the full taste of the steak, there is no other way. If you can't stand the sight of blood, man up, carnivore! Think about it - you like pink, right? I mean think of it as THAT, if it helps. Do whatever you have to do to learn to enjoy medium-done. If you still can't stomach it, skip to the next section.

For you remaining Big Swinging Dicks (BSDs), we salute you, and we are going to tell you how to really DO your meat.   First, you are going to jump down to our "Brine a Lot" recipe on page 44 and prepare your meat. It'll take at least an hour. Stop whining. If you were waiting to get laid, you wouldn't bitch over an hour wait, so don't start now. Go find a video or something. Don't forget to wash your hands afterwards.

After you have finished marinating your meat, fire up your grill. What? No grill? Damn, fried steak is just not quite as good, but if the gods only gave you four inches, well, you make do with what you've got, right? See the Steak au Poivre (Peppercorn steak) on page 46. Adjust the grill/stove to medium heat, or, if you're using coals, place the steak slightly to the side of the hottest part of the coals. Put your steak on the grill and leave it. Resist farting around with it. After two minutes or so, rotate the steak 90 degrees on the grill without flipping it. On thicker steaks, sear for three minutes before rotating. This will give you nice cross-hatched grill marks. After another 2 to 3 minutes, flip the steak. DO NOT USE A FORK TO TURN OR FLIP, lest you be an asshat, and ruin the steak. Use tongs. Allow the steak to cook for another 2 to 3 minutes. Rotate it 90 degrees and cook for another 2 to 3 minutes. If you cook your meat for much more than 12 minutes total, go back to tofu.

Meat Poking Test

Since we assume you can figure out the OTHER poking yourself, we're going to teach you how to touch-test your meat so you don't overcook it. Open your hand and push your finger against the pad of your hand that is at the base of your thumb. If you push your finger against the steak and it rebounds like that, it's raw. Cook it longer. Now, put your index finger and thumb together to make the "okay" sign. Poke the pad at the base of your thumb again. That's rare. Yum! Your middle finger and thumb is medium-rare, ring finger and thumb is Medium, and the pinkie finger and thumb is Well Done.

If the steak feels right using the poke-test, pull that bad-boy off the grill or pan. Now here's something REALLY effin' important. Do NOT cut into the steak yet. Steak, like you after a good bonk, needs a rest. Let it. Put the steak on a plate, or a clean cutting board, and let it rest. Five minutes. No exceptions. If you cut it, or poke it with a knife or thermometer, or whatever stupid idea you have for violating its steaky integrity, all the juices will drain out, and you will have dry meat.

Now when you cut open the steak, look at the inside. If it's half pink or more, you win! If it's all red, well we admire your manliness, but that's called steak tartare (raw steak) and you may be a better man than we if you eat it anyway. Go ahead and throw the steak on the grill again, only turn it up. If the steak is all brown, well, you jacked up and you either need to control your fire, caveman, or you need to rotate the steak and flip it a little sooner next time. In other words, shorten the cooking time.

Assuming you did not fail us, you should have an exceptional steak. You'll hopefully have checked out the "Wingmen" section for excellent baked potatoes, or whatever, to go with it.

Beat your meat: Medium-Well to Well-Done

Now there are some people that will cook a steak past medium. We are not those people. If you are going to do that, you are an abomination unto us and you will offend the gods. We will tell you what to do to try to make the best of it, but there's something seriously wrong with you. First off, don't waste your money on really good cuts; you're going to ruin them. A middlin' cut of beef or even crap beef will do for the likes of you. Go to the store and buy a bottle of "Meat Tenderizer" in the spice or meat section. Now go to your garage and pick up a hammer. Kidding, don't actually do that! You're actually going to go to the store and get the other "meat tenderizer," which looks like a flat headed hammer with a diamond pattern on the striking face of the hammer. It is a unitasker, but it is needed since you insist on abusing your meat. If you are NOT going to use our "Brine a Lot" marinade recipe below, then coat the steak with some olive oil and sprinkle the Meat Tenderizer salt on the steak and beat the ever-loving HELL out of it with the meat hammer. Really work out those Boss-issues on the steak. If the steak goes flat, well you have "Carne Asada" and it should be good no matter how "well-done" you cook it.

If you don't want to spend the money on the Meat Hammer of Thor, then take out a simple fork and fork it. No really, fork the shit out of it. Fork it hard. Lots of forking. Fork it good. It should be so full of holes it'll look like the Gatling gun in *Predator* opened up on the steak.

Now that you have prepared the meat, it's time to ruin it. Slap that bad boy on the grill, or even fry it in a pan. Probably won't matter. Cook it on one side for about 10 minutes. Cook it on the other until it doesn't spring back when you poke it with a finger. You've gone and well-done it. Don't worry about letting it sit. It is ready to eat. In a manner of speaking. It should be barely edible.

Now that we have explained "well-done" steak to you, keep in mind that when you don't feel like cooking and go to a restaurant and order "well-done," the chef will literally not give a cow's crap about your steak. It's not her fault. You are clearly beneath her, and not in the way you want to be.

Brine A Lot? Meat Marinade

Soundtrack: *Yellow Submarine* by the Beatles

Men, have you got a grill yet? No? Do you walk around with one testicle often? Okay then, go get one! A grill that is, not a testicle. Hopefully you came pre-equipped with those. Thomas did not go to all this trouble to come up with this kick-ass marinade brine to have you all walk around minus one ball. Obtain some decent GEAR and get it now, because you're gonna need to cook up some meat. No, not chicken. MEAT. Beef. Preferably of a size and heft that would make a sumo wrestler pale trying to eat it all. You want marbled beef (that's FAT for you waifs). You do NOT want that underfed skinny nonfat beef that you find served in Hollyweird, which the Melrose Place people smell, and then feed to the dog because they're "watching their figure." Waaaah. Get real meat with some fat on it. Trim the excess fat before you apply the marinade. Place the meat in a sealable bag and add the following ingredients:

Bottle of good ginger ale
Splash of wine (red or white)
Big pinch of kosher salt
Tablespoon of honey or molasses
Splash of raspberry vinegar OR lemon/lime juice (fresh squeezed)

Splash of Worcestershire sauce
Teaspoon of mustard
Fresh ground black pepper

First, a word about balance; when you are cooking, it helps to learn to balance flavors: sweet, salt, bitter, sour, and savory. We almost left out measurements on this recipe to force you to think about it. We gave you a starting point to experiment with, but it is by no means a fixed recipe. Live on the edge, add some extra this or that to taste. Really, tiger, you can do it. What flavors above sound good with steak? All of them, right? Now which might overpower the steak and make it too...salty? Too sweet? Too sour?

The ginger ale is sweet, but it's a mild sweet, and mainly a base for the other flavors. You might want to go easier on the stronger flavors like the Worcestershire and the salt. Raspberry vinegar does two things for your marinade, it provides flavor, but it also provides acid (the vinegar) as a meat tenderizer. Other acids include lemon or lime juice. Wine also acts as a tenderizer, and provides robust flavor as well.

Dijon mustard is THE stuff. We prefer the Grey one. Yeah, yeah, we know the damn Frenchies invented it, but hell, they also seem get laid more than any other country. Think about it.

You will want to mix up a batch of the marinade in a big bowl, and as you add ingredients, taste it. If it tastes too strong or too bland, add ingredients to compensate. Start with the ginger ale, and then add to it, to taste. When you have a flavor you like, put the liquid into a big sealable plastic bag that will hold the marinade and the steak.

Let the steak fridge-soak in the marinade for one to four hours, turning the bag over in the fridge periodically if necessary to keep it soaking in the liquids. The marinade works only if it is in contact with the steak. If you're one of those impatient types, you can probably get away with one hour, but then you could also wear your girlfriend's bikini. We don't recommend it. After the steaks have marinated, take the steaks out of the bag and fire up that grill. Heat the grill up to 300 degrees or so, and start the sizzling.

Again, listen up; do NOT cook it "well done." Yeah, I know, you don't want all that blood. Boo hoo. It's MEAT. So cook it medium. Tops. You won't regret it.

Whatever you do, do NOT be a numbnut and slice the meat on the grill to check it for dumbness, err, done-ness. A thick 2-inch steak will take about 6 to 8 minutes on a side, or LESS. When you're cooking the steak, cook one side for 2 to 3 minutes at an angle to the grill, then 2-3 minutes on the same side at a 90-degree angle to get hash marks.

When you turn the steak, do the same 2 minute, 90-degree, 3 minute trick, then pull the steak off the grill. Now again for the impatient ones that can't keep from premature..... WAIT, dammit. You need to let that steak rest for 5 minutes. If you go and pop off prematurely by cutting the steak, you'll lose all the juices and go limp. We wouldn't want THAT to happen. Let the steak rest for FIVE minutes. Bon Appesteak!

Get your Brine Game on...

So you read this at work when you should have been, well, working. Now you are all hot and bothered for some steak. No worries. For the first timers out of the gate, go to the grocery store and pick up a box of sealable bags. Swing over to the spice section and get one of those picnic packs of salt and pepper. We know this is cheating, but you haven't given us much to work with. Brace yourself. Pick up a 12 ounce bottle of grocery store marinade, preferably one with lime. Swing over to the soda aisle and grab a bottle of seltzer or ginger ale. Hit the meat counter and ask the nice lady behind the counter for a great cut of beef, pork, or salmon. Pay and head to your hot rod. Open up all the stuff you just bought, put the meat in a sealable bag, shake in some pepper, pour salt in your hand till the little pile is about half an inch across in your cupped palm, and toss that in the bag. Add about a third of the bottle of marinade, and pour in all the seltzer. Close it up with as little air as you can manage without shooting the meat out onto the parking lot. Place the bag in the passenger seat, note the time, and head home. If anyone stares while you are doing all this (and they will), just smile smugly as you are already brining dinner while they are staring at a monkey in the parking lot.

Steak au Poivre (Peppercorn steak)

Soundtrack: *Push It* by Salt-N-Pepa

2 thick USDA select steaks	2 Tablespoons cracked Tellicherry black peppercorns
Butter or olive oil	2 cloves of garlic
1 Tablespoon minced shallots	2 Tablespoons brandy or cognac
½ cup red wine	½ cup heavy cream

You are going to need to crack the peppercorns, yet also not have them fly everywhere. The best way is with a mortar and pestle; however, you can also place the peppercorns into a plastic bag and crack them with a rolling pin, or by tapping very lightly with a hammer. Mr. Gear Head, if you use the hammer from your garage, clean the damn oily thing first, capiche? Also, be aware of the surface you are pounding on. You do not want to dent or break the kitchen counter, and have your spouse beat you to death with your meat hammer.

Remove the cracked peppercorns from the bag and press them firmly into both sides of the steaks with your hands. Heat the butter or olive oil in a heavy skillet, then sear the steaks on high heat 'til browned. Reduce the heat to medium and cook to medium-doneness (see page 43). You should only have to flip the steak once, and you DO NOT want to use a fork to do it. Use tongs or a wooden spoon. Remove the steak from the pan with the tongs, plate it, and let the steak rest for FIVE minutes before you so much as show it to a knife or fork, no exceptions.

Leaving the steak juices in the pan, add shallots and garlic to pan and sauté, stirring occasionally, until the shallots go from purple-y white to clear. Add brandy and wine, and then boil while stirring for three to four minutes or so to reduce the sauce and thicken it a little. Reduce the heat a little more and add the heavy cream to the pan and let it slowly heat until the sauce is warmed again. Pour sauce over steaks. Enjoy!

Roast Beast

Soundtrack: *Hella Good* by No Doubt

If you are ready for some serious meat, you just can't do better than a nice pot roast. You are, however, gonna need a pot with a lid, and it needs to be a big one. If you are a serious gearhead and willing to spend money, the Le Creuset pots are absolutely awesome.[75] Yes, the orange and red one that looks like the flames on a 55 Chevy is what we are talking about. Crazy cool gear. If you are a "special needs" cook in the kitchen, we actually recommend a slow cooker "crock pot" for this effort.

First we will tell you the safe crock pot way, then we'll tell you the manly Le Creuset way later. Note preparation time of 5 to 10 hours required! But it IS worth it.

---

[75] Le Creuset pots are breakup pots; when you have to break up with her, make sure you have those pots in hand BEFORE the fireworks start.

With a beef roast, size *does* matter, so you need to buy one that will fit in your crock pot. You're gonna want to brine the roast, so mix up the Brine-a-Lot Meat Marinade on page 44, bag it up, and off you go. You'll want to have it set in the brine for about an hour for each pound of beef.

Olive oil	Red potatoes
2 onions	10 garlic cloves
3 fresh carrots	Bunch of green onions
1 leek	Package of dry onion soup mix

3 cups stock or broth, soup, or a little wine will work here

Grab your leek and clean it VERY well of dirt. She won't want gritty bits in her food and neither will you. First cut off the green ends that are really tough and inedible. Now, set the leek on your cutting board and cut it lengthwise, starting at the roots and cutting to the green end. You now have two long halves, take them and carefully wash the dirt out, starting at the white ends letting the water run down through the green end and out. Now put the leek on your board and slice the leek into little half-ringlets. Cut the potatoes into halves and then quarters. Slice the onions thinly, then peel and cut the carrots up into bite-sized pieces. See www.manmeetstove.com/videoz and click on the "Knife Skillz" video for tips on how to do this without losing your digits. You'll need them later for more activities. Or so we hope.

Take the dried skin off five garlic cloves and toss them into the pot whole, as well as five garlic cloves that have been sliced up. Cut the root and white part off the green onions. Cut the remaining green ends into inch-long pieces and add them to the mix. Save the whites for something else, or compost them. Add soup mix and about half of the liquids to the slow cooker.

Add a pat of butter to the pot, heat up the frying pan to *very* hot, then throw the roast into the pan. You want the roast to brown on all sides, but try not to burn it. Set the roast into the cooker and add the remaining liquid, cover and cook for about 200 hours. Actually, it should take about 6 to 8 hours on low for a 6-pound roast to get to the point that the meat is falling-apart tender. Eat it right out of the cooker with a fork and a jar of mayonnaise. Actually, only do that if your Special Friend isn't there.

If you don't have a crock pot, mostly follow all the same instructions, only you can brown the roast in the large Le Creuset lidded pot. After the roast is browned, lift the roast out of the pot, add in the vegetables, and place the meat back on top, so it sits off the bottom of the pot on the veggies. Put the lid on, and set the pot over a very low heat to cook. You're gonna have to watch it a little, though. If your liquids boil off, make sure the lid is on tight, turn the heat down, and add a little more water or broth. Cook for 3 ½ to 4 hours. Enjoy.

Leftover roast beast is seriously good remnants. Makes killer sandwiches. She should enjoy this with you for days after you make it. Cold or hot. The roast beast that is.

Carne Asada

Soundtrack: *Cabo Wabo* by Van Halen

We like steak and can't imagine why you wouldn't want steak at most any meal. This carne asada is a good all-around meat for all meals of the day. For a pre-dawn post-quickie snack, reheat it, and serve with half an avocado. It goes awesome with any of the egg breakfasts. The lunch tacos you make with this will have those "special people" you call friends drooling. Dinner carne asada with rice and beans is a good start on a classy meal out, but you are staying in.

Preparation time of 1 to 4 hours required!

1 lemon, 1 lime, and 1/2 an orange   1/2 cup minced cilantro
3 to 5 cloves of garlic, minced   Teaspoon Mexican oregano
Pinch of ground cumin seed   Pinch of salt and black pepper, to taste
Taco-sized corn or flour tortillas   Teaspoon ground coriander seed (don't overdo this)

1 or 2 serrano chilies, minced (be a big boy and use them both; you already bought them!)

Optional: Mexican cerveza or tequila; refried beans; mayonnaise; lettuce; lime; tomato; avocado

There is a good range of meat you can use for carne asada, and if you are pinching Penny, err, pennies, use a pound of flank or skirt steak. If you're using cheapo steak, you may want to use a meat hammer as described on page 44. If you're splurging on Penny, get her the top sirloin.

Whip out your steak into a small bowl. Squeeze the juice from a lemon, a lime, and half an orange over the steak. If you don't have a juicer, simply slice the citrus in half and squeeze it over your cupped hand over the steak. As the juice and seeds fall into your cupped hand, open your fingers just barely enough so the juice dribbles through, but the seeds are caught between your fingers. This kind of finger dexterity skills will benefit you in other areas, so practice, practice, practice! After the juice drains through your fingers, throw away the seeds. Repeat until all the fruit juices are added to the steak in the bowl. If you want to kick it up a notch, add some beer or tequila to the lemon juice. Don't forget to sample some for yourself. The beer or tequila that is. The juice is for lightweights.

Now here's a little something you want to check. Some people are allergic to cilantro. Okay, they are not really allergic; they are genetic mutants that do not have the cilantro gene. This is not a joke; they actually genetically despise the stuff, and it tastes like soap to them. So, if you haven't tried cilantro before, take a little taste of it. It will be a strong grassy flavor, uncooked. If you are like us, you won't be able to get enough of it after you try it. But you may want to check with your guests. Just ask them if they don't like certain greens; they will usually know which they despise.

If you can take the heat, dice up a Serrano pepper and add it to the steak. If you can't, then for Penny's sake at least, add in a mild pepper like a Poblano pepper, seeded and diced. Pour in two glugs[76] of olive oil, slice 3 to 5 garlic cloves, and throw it into the mix (don't forget to peel the dry skins off the garlic, lest you look like a tool, and your food taste like it). Finely chop half the cilantro and throw into the steak bowl with all the rest of the spices listed, EXCEPT the salt. Stir the steaks so they are all well coated with the spicy citrus juice mixture. You want the steaks to look all glossy and wet like a....well....wet.

Cover the bowl of steaks in the marinade with plastic wrap and stick it in the fridge. Let it soak for at least an hour, preferably four. Do not marinade for much more than that, or the citrus will destroy the meat into mush.

---

[76] A technical term: more than a splash, and less than a bucket.

If you have a grill or a broiler under your stove, it's man time. If you have any women-folk around, send them off to pick flowers or something, because we are going to play with fire, and that's man business. If they give you any lip, just remind them that YOU are cooking. Yes, YOU, need you say more? Women are generally smarter than we are, and certainly smarter than you are, so that should clear the room for you to focus on the fire.

Wire brush the grill to clean it, and preheat it. When the grill is ready, you can brush on a little oil. Whatever you do, do not use a spray-oil, as it will become a flame thrower, or worse. Don't even think about it unless you want to look like Conan the chubby idiot with no eyebrows. Take the steaks out of the marinade, salt them, and grind on some black pepper. Grill, or broil, the steaks for six minutes on a side, turning over ONLY once during the cooking. You're looking for medium rare. After both sides have cooked for six minutes, remove from the grill or broiler. We know it looks and smells good and that you want to just bite into the steak-y goodness right away, but just like being with a fine woman, you need to take your time! Set the steak on a cutting board and let it REST for five minutes. Yes, five whole minutes. It holds in all those luscious juices. After the resting period is over, you can now cut it diagonally into long strips. If you cooked it right, you should see a luscious pink layer in the center of the strips. We LIKE pink. Right?

Carne asada is good grub just as it is. Plate it and eat it. We like it with a helping of cooked beans covered with grated cheddar cheese. Rice is also a nice wingman for the carne asada.

Carne asada also makes a very mean "Torta" steak sandwich. Get a Kaiser roll, white burger bun, or some other favorite bread, and spread a liberal portion of mayonnaise, followed by crushed avocado on one slice of the bread. Spread some warm refried beans over the other slice of bread. Add lettuce, cheese, tomatoes, and squeeze a lime over it. Eat.

If you want to make carne asada tacos, go to pages 17 and 48 and follow the recipe. Don't forget to squeeze some lime wedges over the tacos. Good grub.

Liberate some of those cervezas or shots of tequila and serve them with the carna asada. Go easy there, tiger, that tequila may not help your performance later. After she loves your cooking, she might want to love on you.

Melange BBQ Rub

Soundtrack: *Main Theme from the Motion Picture "Dune"* by Toto

1 cup brown sugar	½ cup sweet Hungarian paprika
2 Tablespoons coarse ground black pepper	2 Tablespoons cup white pepper
2 Tablespoons lemon pepper	2 Tablespoons cup granulated garlic
2 Tablespoons onion powder	¼ cup Kosher salt
¼ cup chili powder	¼ cup cumin
2 Tablespoons cayenne	

He who controls the universe, must know how to use the spice. – Thomas and Jim

If you want to make great barbeque, you're gonna need a good spice rub. You're really gonna need a lot more than spice alone if you want to be the God Emperor of competition BBQ, but the rub is a good starting point.

Mix all the spice together, and sprinkle it all over a pork butt, rack of ribs, or even a beef roast. You're going to want to slow roast/barbeque the meats. Go easy on the spice there, Sparky, if you're dealing with ribs. You can go hog wild with a roast.

Tip:
Pork butt is actually the front shoulder. Go figure. The ham is the actual pig butt.

If you want to get serious about barbeque, you should experiment with the spice a bit. Decreasing the sugar on big roasts of meat, for example, might be a good idea. You can add different kinds of chili pepper, including ancho chili powder and chipotle chili powder. You are limited only by your imagination. Remember, it's okay to walk[77] without rhythm.

Vegetarian Meatloaf
For the One Night Stand with the Hippie Chick Vegetarian

Soundtrack: *I'm Too Sexy* by Right Said Fred

Everyone needs a one hit wonder. This is yours. When you are approaching the sandal and hemp-clad beauty, you will need more than just a salad to feed her. Taking her to a steak house because they have a "great potato bar" is just lame. This shows you're reaching into her world.

Half a box Special K cereal	Little tub cottage cheese (16 oz)	6 eggs
¼ cup olive oil	Onion	Garlic
Basil and oregano (fresh, preferably)	Spaghetti sauce	Cheddar cheese
Packet of onion or vegetable soup mix		

Get out the big bowl, dump in the cereal, cottage cheese, oil, and crack the eggs (into a separate bowl), and add them to the mix once you have fished out the egg shell remnants. Mix with a wooden spoon. Dice up the onion and toss it into a small frying pan with some butter. When the onion starts to turn clear, pour into the bowl with the cereal and eggs. Tear open the soup mix and pour it in. Mix. Smell it again. Add basil and oregano until it starts to smell like the herbs instead of the egg and cottage cheese. Dice the garlic and mix it in.

Butter up the bottom and sides of a baking dish. A 9x12 inch dish will do, but anything close will work. Scrape the bowl out into the baking dish. Use the back of the wooden spoon to smooth it out and get the mixture to an even depth.

---

[77] Like an Egyptian

Bake at 325° for 20 minutes. Pull it out, spread the spaghetti sauce over the top, and put it back in the oven for another 10 minutes. Pull it out of the oven again, sprinkle with shredded cheese, and stuff it back in the oven for a final 10 minutes. If you went with a larger baking dish, you will need to watch it very carefully for the last 15 minutes so you don't burn it. Cut it like a meat loaf, and serve.

Repeat as needed for bootie calls.

Chili: Hot, Meaty Goodness

Soundtrack: *Give It Away* by Red Hot Chili Peppers

We are not all fond of beans. And while we like stew, the brown glop reminds us a bit too much of dormitory / cafeteria food. Chili is the cure for the common bean. You can spend just about as much cash as you want to on this. It's more bucks if you buy good meat, cheese, and sausage. You know we do.

This recipe will serve eight people or four guys like us. Maybe.

Small can of black beans	Small can of Italian spiced tomatoes
2 small cans of tomato juice	Small can of corn (optional)
Pound of ground hamburger (get the 70/30)	Small package of tri-tip steak
Spicy Italian sausage	2 or 3 fresh tomatoes if you have them
Potato	Onion
2 garlic cloves	4 tablespoons corn meal or polenta

Black pepper, chili powder, cayenne pepper, paprika
Fresh hot peppers (put in whatever you think you can take; don't blame us)

Chop the onion and toss some of it into a tall pot. Cook over medium heat with olive oil 'til the onions turn clear. Add the ground cow and some of the garlic and stir it round a bit to break the burger into small pieces. When the burger is just browned, add in the other cans of stuff, and stir. That is basically dormitory chili, with the exception of the fresh ground beef. Dormitory chili uses a can of corned beef hash instead. Do NOT let us catch you slummin' like that.

To dress the chili up and impress those primates you call friends, scrub the hell out of the potato's skin, chop it up, and toss it into the pot, peel and all. Chop the sausage into chunks and stir the tubesteak[78] into the chili pot. Add in the corn meal and spices. Turn the heat way down, maybe all the way to low. Stir occasionally. If the chili gets too thick, add the second can of tomato juice. You can always boil it off later; just remember to stir it occasionally so it doesn't stick to the bottom of the pot and burn.

While the chili is simmering, dribble some olive oil into a 12-inch frying pan. Add in the remaining onion that you saved out earlier and cook over a medium heat. When the onion starts to go clear, stand back and pour in the chopped fresh chilis, remaining garlic, and the tri-tip. Stir that goodness around the pan while the trip-tip browns. If anyone tries to take a forkful of the tri-tip, fend the invader off with a wooden spoon. Try not to leave any marks though.[79]

A little after the tri-tip has browned, shove all that meaty hotness out of the frying pan into the pot, and let the whole thing simmer for half an hour, stirring occasionally. Eat. Enjoy.

---

[78] Not YOUR tubesteak; that would leave a mark!
[79] On second thought, brand them as thieves.

Bison Balls

Strap on your spurs, set the 10-gallon hat wherever it will fit, and let's make some meat balls, Partner.

Ground bison (use ground beef if you must, comrade)
2 or 3 slices of sourdough bread (day-old stale bread is good here)
Liquid (water, broth, or even beer)
Handful of shredded Cheese (start with Jack, Jack)
Chipotle pepper (seeded)

Onion	Bell pepper
Chili powder	Cumin
Coriander	Brown sugar (just a pinch or two)
Pasta sauce or enchilada sauce	Salt and black pepper

Get out the big bowl and wash your hands...with soap and HOT water...for a while. Pull the chef's knife out of the sheath at your side, or out of the knife block. Don't even *think* about storing that fine piece of American steel, recycled by Japan, then engineered and made into a knife by Germans, in a drawer.[80] Remove the seeds from the peppers, dice them up, and toss them in a frying pan with some butter. Dice the onion and add it in with the peppers to warm them up. When they start to smell really good, pour them all into a bowl. Chop the bread until it is quite small, crumbs really. Add the bread crumbs to the bowl. Dump the meat into the bowl and get your hands in there and mash it up. Add the shredded cheese. Turn on the oven to broil, or have a guest do it. Their hands should be less covered in raw meat.

Add some liquid; the mixture should be moist, but not so wet that it flows like water. If you make a ball and stand it on the board, it should stay a ball. A word about the liquid - use water if it is all you have. Anything else will be better, even Dr. Pepper. We give high scores for red wine (a California variety, if you please), ginger ale, beer, or even lemon-lime soda. While we haven't tried it with Red Bull, we are guessing it would still have more flavor than if you just use water. Add a pinch (or two) of the spices to the meat, and go easy on the Coriander as it can take over the world if you let it. Smell it. If it smells good, it will be good. Add a double pinch of the brown sugar and add salt and pepper. Broil until the outside of each ball is slightly brown. Use a fork to roll them over and broil some more. Bust out your sauce from page 69, or, if you are a lazy dog, use Prego or canned enchilada sauce. Add the red sauce and simmer at least 20 more minutes. A word about ball size. If you have huge balls,[81] they will take more time to broil and will more likely be undercooked. If they are tiny,[82] they will burn too easy in the broiler. So keep the balls golf ball size, or a little bigger, but not as big as a tennis ball. If yours are as big as a bull's balls...well, while we appreciate your zeal, don't do that.

---

[80] A proper knife should be displayed like a trophy girlfriend. Sure, it's fun to keep to yourself, but it's better if everyone knows you have it.
[81] Well done, big guy.
[82] Be sure to overcompensate with a nice car...

chicken and other vegetables

A Word about Cock

Those of us that have mastered the culinary arts are rather fond of our red meat. But occasionally something gets in the way, or a more delicate meat is required for a dish, and we have to settle for chicken. Okay, actually, it's not that way at all. Chicken is actually quite tasty, if done properly. It's not duck, or turkey, and certainly not goose. But, hell, let's face it, why does everything "taste like chicken?" Because chicken IS pretty average. However, if you try some of these recipes, well, we'll help you elevate a common clucker into a fabulous...chick.

If you eat out a lot, and not at the Colonel, you will note that chicken seems to come only in breast form, and maybe the odd buffalo wing. While we are big fans of breasts (who isn't?), and have been known to leave a pile of spicy bones in a dive bar or twenty, there actually is a whole bird out there waiting to be cooked up. Jim actually prefers the drumstick and thighs. Yes, we are still talking about chicken. The legs and thighs are often more flavorful, juicy, and tolerant of cooking.

Go out and buy yourself the best bird you can afford. Yes, we mean BIRD. Whole chicken. Why let someone else cut it up only give you some of the pieces? This way you get the whole hen and you might get some good bits extra, known as the giblets. Yes, they are good. If you are a fan of liver, chicken liver pate is just about as good as licking the entire leg of a....well let's just say it's damn good!

Before you get the chicken out, read out section on handling meat and sanitation, page 10. Chicken is very germy stuff, raw.

When you get the chicken, the first thing you should note is there is a front end and a back end. Cavities. Holes. The front end is the bigger one, and there should be some goodies in there for you; they may be in a bag. The bag contains the giblets; pull them out, and set them aside. Don't forget to do this, or it will be a mess later while cooking.

Notice that the wings are naturally positioned towards the bottom front of the bird. They are placed right above and alongside the breasts. Breasts are widely regarded as the best part of the bird, so notice their location. The bottom back of the bird has the drumsticks, which are attached to the thighs. All of these pieces are good to know location-wise as you will be cutting them off at some point. If you are cooking the whole bird, cutting them off will come later; if you are cooking up the pieces, let's get to it.

Chicken Go Pow

Soundtrack: *Hot Stuff* by Donna Summer

Chicken is a blank canvas, (like a coed the week before spring break), and today we are painting our kitchen Picasso. Start this recipe the day before you want to eat it.

Whole chicken (get the nice lady at the meat counter to chop it up in pieces if you can't)

1 gallon warm water	lime
¾ cup kosher salt	⅔ cup sugar
¾ cup soy sauce	¼ cup olive oil
24 ounces of plain Greek yogurt	3 jalapeño peppers
Fresh sage	Cumin
Black pepper	
Bottle of store bought "tamarind lime marinade"	
Hot sauce (Mexican, Chinese, Wing sauce, Louisiana style, or other hot sauce)	

Read the instructions for handling raw chicken safely on page 10. Begin to brine by finding a container or bag large enough to hold the gallon of warm water and the chicken pieces, but small enough to fit in your fridge. You are going to need some Kosher salt, and if you only have table salt, you are going to need to make sure it is NOT iodized salt. If you use table salt, decrease the salt to ½ cup. Mix the warm water, salt, soy sauce, and olive oil in your container until dissolved, then add the chicken pieces, cover with plastic wrap or lid, and put in the fridge for at least 4 hours.

After the chicken has fully marinated, pre-heat your grill on high. Put a cup and a half of plain Greek yogurt in a small bowl. Take the seeds and white pulp out of the middle of three jalapeño peppers, chop the peppers up small, and add them to the yogurt. Add in a few shakes of cumin, black pepper, and fresh sage. Give it a mix with a spoon and then add in a quarter cup of a tamarind lime marinade. Add a few good shots of hot sauce (try to find a bottle that has almost no English on it; better still if it has a wooden cap), mix and taste. The sauce should be tangy and hot. If it is missing the tang, add a squeeze of lime. If it is not hot, go for some more of the hot sauce.

Set up your counter to deal with the chicken. Raw chicken is a Grim Reaper of bacteria so always use a dedicated chicken cutting board. Set the bowl of marinade to the side of the board. Beyond that, have a special platter that you will use to take the meat to the grill. Set the bag of chicken and brine in the sink on the opposite side of the board from the marinade bowl. Wash your meat paws, Quasimodo, and then begin.

Open the container and drain the salt bath away until you can grab a piece of chicken. Set each piece of chicken out on the board to dry, being careful to watch out not to cut yourself on edges of bone, as they are sharp. If you cut yourself on a bone, you will live to regret it. Or you may not live.

It's time to position your chicken bits. Working as cleanly as you can, slather each piece of chicken in the marinade. For the bigger pieces, just set them in the marinade sauce, wiggle them around, and flip them over.[83] Once all the chunks of chicken are coated and on your platter, head out to the grill. Throw away the remaining marinade sauce. Wash your hand THOROUGHLY with hot, soapy water for several minutes, unless you want to spend the next three days paying homage to the porcelain god. Same for all your dishes and utensils. Dishwasher is best if you've got one. A good final quick rinse with vinegar is also recommended.

Oil the grill grate by pouring some olive oil onto a folded paper towel and wiping over the grate. Use your tongs to keep from burning your precious pinkies. Toss the chicken pieces onto the grill. Here's the fun part; different chicken pieces require different cooking times. Let's start with the breasts.[84] Grill the chicken breasts for two minutes, rotate 90 degrees (using tongs, NOT a fork), and cook for another 2 to 4 minutes. Turn the breasts over and repeat the grilling process: two minutes, rotate, two to four more minutes. The total grilling time for breasts is 4 to 6 minutes per side. Drumsticks and thighs need to go through the same drill, only 8 to 10 minutes total per side. If you have trouble with two girls at once, you may want to cook all the breasts first, then the drumsticks and thighs. We understand.

---

[83] Do not move your body while doing this. That is dancing, and not what we are here for.
[84] It's called "foreplay"…

Fiery Chicken Fingers

Soundtrack: *Hot Hot Hot* by Buster Poindexter

Chicken fingers made with this recipe look good in addition to tasting great! If you are trying to reduce that beer gut, then these are your hot ticket. Literally.

> 2 pounds boneless skinless chicken breasts (5 to 6 breast halves)
> Olive oil

MARINADE and DIPPING SAUCE:

1/2 cup picante sauce	2 tablespoons honey	1 teaspoon ground cumin

Read the instructions for handling raw chicken safely on page 10. Cut the chicken breasts on your chicken-specific cutting board into 1 inch wide strips. Set aside. Mix the marinade ingredients in a shallow dish, and set aside a little in a separate bowl in the refrigerator. Place the chicken in the marinade, cover, and refrigerate for several hours, or overnight. Preheat your oven to 400 degrees. Coat a rectangular broiling pan with oil. Place the marinated chicken strips in a single layer in the pan, and baste[85] with half of the sauce. Place the chicken on the top oven rack for 5 minutes. Turn the strips over, and bake for an additional 3 minutes, or until the chicken is fork-tender and no longer pink inside.[86] Pull out the second bowl of marinade from the fridge for a dipping sauce. Note: Do NOT use the marinade that touched raw chicken as a dipping sauce.[87]

Apricot Chicken, or, How to Get Laid

Soundtrack: *Always on my Mind* by the Pet Shop Boys

4 Chicken breasts	Olive oil	Garlic cloves
24 dried apricots	2 teaspoon Dijon mustard	½ cup apricot or white wine
½ cup soy sauce	½ cup brown sugar	6 Tablespoons honey
Optional – ½ cup apricot nectar		
Optional - ½ teaspoon dried chili pepper flakes (add in for extra heat) or a pinch of Cayenne.		

Go get yourself a date.

In case we didn't mention it, we do like breasts. This is pretty much universal, but is also true with regards to chicken. Set up your gal-pal in the next room with a romance novel and get your cook on. What, you don't have a romance novel? Riiiiight. Okaaaay.

Read the instructions for handling raw chicken safely on page 10. Crush the garlic cloves with the flat side of your chef's knife (carefully, keep the sharp edge down! Do NOT cut yourself, lest your date associates your ability to wield a knife with your ability to wield something else), peel off the dry skin, and slice the cloves. Four garlic cloves or so should be sufficient.

Wash the breasts in the sink. The chicken breasts. Don't get distracted on us now. If there is skin, remove it with a short, sharp paring knife or filet knife. Cut the breasts into strips, removing any excess fat as you go. In a large

---

[85] Think of "basting" as slathering sunscreen all over your girl with a paint brush. Don't use a dirty paintbrush. A dirty girl is preferred.
[86] Make your own pink joke here.
[87] Ever. Be careful not to touch anything you're about to eat that also touched raw chicken.

frying pan, add olive oil and place in the chicken. Using medium heat, cook the breasts until the strips are no longer pink, but still moist and soft, turning occasionally to ensure both sides are cooked. Remember, control your fire, we know there's a girl in the other room, but now's not the time to get all excited and lose your cool. Add oil occasionally, if necessary, to ensure things stay moist in the pan. Add drinks occasionally to ensure things stay moist in the other room. Remove the chicken from the pan and place it onto a temporary plate.

You are going to make your apricot teriyaki in the same frying pan, so don't clean that pan! Add the garlic to the pan, with a little oil, and sauté the garlic for a few minutes, stirring so the garlic doesn't burn. Pour in the soy sauce, wine, optional apricot nectar, brown sugar, Dijon mustard, bay leaf, apricots, and honey. If you are using lite soy sauce (!) add 50% more soy sauce. Stir and scrape the chicken bits off the side of the pan into the liquids. Keep stirring occasionally while cooking. You want to cook and reduce the liquids until they turn into a thick sauce, called a glaze. Reduce the heat once you have your glaze, since you don't want to burn it. Remove the bay leaf, and add the cooked chicken back into the glaze. Stir the chicken around for a couple of minutes until well coated with the apricot teriyaki glaze/sauce and then plate it.

This dish has always been popular with the ladies. We like to eat it over rice with a side of broccoli. Serve it up with a nice glass of wine, and wit. If you haven't got the latter, well, give her more wine.

Green Soup

Soundtrack: *It's Not Easy Being Green* by Kermit the Frog

The chopping in this recipe is quite a bit of work, but what man doesn't enjoy playing with knives? The great soup makes it worth the work. If you have a vegan or vegetarian lass, this should at least get you to second base. Probably farther than that, assuming you've been paying attention to what we say here.

You're gonna need an hour or two to do this, so throw "The Notebook," "You've Got Mail," or another happy chick flick into the player while you cook. Remember to occasionally bring her a glass of wine for lubrication, and a blanket to wrap up in. Set the stage for the bliss to come...

2 large bunches Swiss chard (or spinach)	6 cloves garlic, finely chopped
2 bunches kale (green leaves only)	9 cups water
3 cups cilantro, loosely packed	3 large potatoes
Salt	4 onions, chopped
Olive oil	Freshly ground black pepper
6 cups vegetable or chicken broth[88]	Juice of one lemon juice, more to taste
Dash cayenne pepper	
Optional: Heavy cream, Feta cheese, wine	

Wash the greens thoroughly, then cut the chard and kale off their stems, and slice or tear the leaves into 2" chunks. Combine the chard, kale, and cilantro in a soup pot with the water and 1 teaspoon of salt. Peel the potatoes, or just scrub them well, cut them into big pieces, and add to the pot. Bring the water to a boil, reduce

---

[88] Like most things, homemade is better, of course

the heat, and let the whole mess simmer for about half an hour. Don't forget to keep your date properly wined while she's been waiting.

Meanwhile, heat a splash of oil in a nonstick skillet. Add the chopped onions and a sprinkle of salt and cook them over low heat until they are golden (caramelized) and soft. This will take up to 45 minutes;[89] don't hurry, you only need to give them a stir once in a while, and it's the slow cooking that develops the sweetness. If you are really bored, go play with your date, just don't get too involved (if you know what we mean) and burn the onions. If you like, you can deglaze[90] the pan at the end with a generous splash of Marsala wine or sherry. Increase the heat to medium, and add the Marsala booze. Return it to the stove and cook the onions, stirring for 1 minute. Add the onions to the soup. Give your date some leftover Marsala you set aside.

Put another splash of oil in the skillet and cook the garlic over low heat, stirring continuously to keep the garlic from burning, until it sizzles and smells great. It will probably take 1 to 2 minutes. Add the garlic to the soup pot and simmer everything for a few minutes more. Give more wine to your date.

At this point there won't be much liquid in the soup, so add enough water - up to an additional 3 cups - to make the soup...a soup. Puree the using a hand blender. You can also use a regular blender, if that is what you have, doing a little bit at a time, as much as your blender will handle. Start the blender slowly and then speed it up, lid tightly on, or you will have hot burning liquid shoot out the top. Wine, date, repeat.

Return the soup to the pot, bring it back to a simmer and taste. Add salt as needed, grind in a little black pepper; add the cayenne and the lemon juice. Stir well and taste again. Now you're on your own; correct the seasoning by adding a little salt, broth, or lemon to taste, and then serve these big steaming bowls of green soup piping hot. By now she may not be able to taste it for the wine...

We like to garnish this soup with feta cheese. Croutons are always good as well, especially if they're home made from rye or pumpernickel bread. Garlic croutons are da bombe, as the kids say. And of course, there's always sour cream, but because we like the low-fat quality of the soup, we use a spoonful of yogurt instead.

Now take those bowls out to your lady friend and pop a tasty crouton into her mouth as you do. We recommend rounding out the meal with a fresh loaf of crusty bakery bread. Use real butter slathered all over the top of it. Tear it with your hands to serve. Butter slathered fingers are a good beginning...

---

[89] If you pay close attention, you can do this in much shorter time over higher heat, but keep it stirring. Don't burn!
[90] A fancy word for using a liquid to remove and dissolve the tasty brown caramelized bits of food from a pan to make a pan sauce.

wingmen

A good cook knows how to add sides that will impress. We know you may need to overcompensate for certain things, so we provide you with the, ahem, tools you may lack...or not, if the gods shone upon you in that department.

Avocado Mounds with Fish

Soundtrack: *Avocado* by Luiz Bonfa.

This is a dish Jim encountered in North Chile called Palta Rellena. It is about as simple as missionary style in a King-sized bed.

3 ripe avocados	Fresh cilantro leaves, chopped
2 cans tuna in water (or two cans of chicken)	4 Tablespoons mayonnaise.
Himalayan pink salt and fresh ground pepper, to taste	Juice of one lemon
Cayenne pepper or Tabasco sauce (optional)	

Crack the cans of tuna open, but leave the lid sitting on top. While holding the lid and the can in a Mr. Miyagi karate pinch, squeeze the fish over the sink as you turn the can sideways to drain off the water, using the lid to keep the tuna in the can. Dump the tuna into a bowl and add the cilantro leaves. Add a little lemon juice, and season with salt and pepper to taste. Add the mayonnaise and toss until well combined.

Tip:
Give a man a fish and you will feed him for a day. Give a fish a man, and you probably work for the mafia.

Follow the directions on the guacamole recipe (page 25) for how to cut open an avocado and remove the pit. Peel the avocados using a small paring knife. Season the inside of the avocado halves with salt and a little bit of lemon juice.

Grab an avocado half and fill the hole with the tuna salad. You can just fill the pit-hole, if you want, but don't be shy if you'd like to cover your 'cado to the edges with tuna. If you want to add an extra special kick, you can very lightly dust with a pinch of cayenne pepper or a drop of Tabasco sauce on top of the tuna salad.

If you're not a big fan of fish flavor, well, we think that there is something wrong with your taste buds. In that case, use cans of chunk chicken instead of the tuna.

T-Man's Righteous Potato Salad

Soundtrack: *Solid Potato Salad* by King Cole Trio

6 large-ish[91] potatoes (red, white, and Yukon gold potatoes)	
6 eggs or 9, knock yourself out[92]	Paprika
1 large sweet onion	Salt and cracked pepper
Green olives (stuffed with garlic)	
Mayonnaise (we use 2 cups if no one is looking, sometimes less if someone is watching her figure)	

Peel and cut the potatoes into small cubes, then boil them in slightly salted water until a fork sticks in easy. Hard boil the eggs, but only just barely as described on page 41. Peel and dice the eggs, making sure to crumble the

---

[91] A technical measurement.

[92] Don't ACTUALLY knock yourself out, unless 1) she isn't there to see it, and 2) there is no one ELSE there to see it. Also, if you DO knock yourself out, don't tell anyone, EVER.

yolks. Put the potatoes and eggs in a large bowl, and add in the mayonnaise. mayonnaise. Cheapo mayo tastes like old eggs and spoiled milk had a bastard child.

Go ahead, put in more mayo, don't be shy. Chop the olives and add them in with a with a big spoon until it all blends together, adding more mayonnaise until the pota the other stuff is about the consistency of sour cream. Taste. Add a little spice ur potato flavor is balanced with the egg.

In a pinch you can use pickle in place of the olive, but not sweet pickles. That's like dipping a supermodel in mud. Okay, maybe not for some of you, since you're into that, but don't put sweet pickles into potato salad.

Mustard? No. You're not trying to impress your grandma's friends.[93] Don't do it. Same goes for vinegar.

Chill for a few hours. You should chill the potato salad too. Serve. It will be even better the next day, so go ahead, make it a double.

BCQ - Blue Cheese Quesedilla

Soundtrack: *Another Way to Die* by Disturbed

If you have a few odd things[94] and a frying pan, you are in for a treat. The sharp flavor of the blue cheese gives some bang to left-over meat. We like this best with left-over burger, or steak.

Leftover meat	Flour tortillas	Blue cheese
Avocado	Salt and Pepper	Fresh basil or oregano
Butter		

If you are a fan of blue cheese, this recipe is for you. If you are not a fan, well, surely you have other talents that somebody wants. Use whatever cheese you like. Just make sure that it melts, like sharp cheddar, for example.

Take a tortilla and place it on a plate. Fry up a fistful of the leftover meat, Salt-N-Pepa to taste, and sprinkle with herbs such as basil or oregano. When the meat is warmed up, crumble some blue cheese onto the tortilla, then dump the meat from the frying pan onto the tortilla. Spread the cheese and meat evenly across the tortilla to form one layer almost from edge to edge. Kill the fire. Don't clean the pan, leave the juices from the meat. You'll be frying in them in a minute.

> **Tip:**
> If someone thinks they have the upper hand, kick them out of your kitchen.

See page 25 for how to prep and cut up an avocado, then lay down a layer of sliced avocado on top of the meat and blue cheese, and place another tortilla on top.

If your frying pan has a nice coating of meat juices, great. If not, pour a little olive oil into the pan and coat the pan evenly with oil. Slide the tortillas, filled with decadent meat and cheese, into the frying pan. Hit the heat again and cook for about for a minute on each side. To flip the quesadilla after the one side is cooked, slide the tortilla out of the pan, onto the plate, place another plate over it, and flip. Slide the quesadilla off the second plate and back into the pan to cook the other side.

Don't burn your tongue. A burnt tongue is an unhappy tongue, and you might want to use that later on her.

---

[93] Unless your into that sort of thing, you kinky devil.
[94] Okay, a few OTHER odd things.

Teutonic Goddess' Umeboshi Vinaigrette OMG Orgasm Salad

k: *Back for More* **by Ratt**

Umeboshi vinegar	"Living" butter lettuce	Olive oil
Garlic (eight cloves)	2 Shallots	Ground pepper

First, you are going to need to run out and find the umeboshi vinegar. It is a Japanese vinegar made from the pickled "ume" plum, and can be found at premium health food markets and Asian/Japanese markets. If you find it, stock up. Three bottles minimum. You never know when there might be a natural disaster and you wouldn't want to be caught with your umebashi down.

The butter lettuce should be available at your local stupormarket.[95] Take the butter lettuce and cut off the bottom (the root ball of the lettuce plant). Rinse the lettuce really well, then pull the leaves apart into smaller pieces with your fingers, placing torn leaves into a big bowl. The lettuce pieces should be about double bite-size, not whole leaf-sized, Rambo. See page 20 on how to properly peel garlic. You'll need to peel the dry skin off the shallots as well. Mince (chop really fine) the garlic and shallots and dump them into a wide-mouthed jar. Those canning jars that your grandma used for jam, with a flat cap and ring, are perfect.[96] You can also use a CLEAN wide-mouthed jar like a small mayo jar that you recycled. Don't even THINK about using a dirty jar; you'll get a wicked case of the galloping doodahs,[97] or worse.

Now pour olive oil into the jar till you have about 2 inches. That's in the bottom of the jar, not that other place where you have 2 inches. Pour some umeboshi vinegar into the jar on top of the olive oil until the total liquids in the jar is about 2½ inches deep. Salad dressing ratio is roughly 1:2, vinegar to oil. Umeboshi vinegar is strong on flavor, so go light. Add the diced shallots and garlic. Seal the jar lid onto the jar and shake the crap out of it. If the lid leaks, you will now have a hellofa mess.[98] No, that laughter is not from us, it's our ringtone.

After the dressing is well shaken, open the jar and take a leaf of butter lettuce and dip it in the dressing. Very salty? Add olive oil. Only tastes like oil? Add umeboshi. Reseal the lid and shake between taste tests,[99] then taste again. Do NOT double dip the lettuce while taste testing; haven't we taught you anything? IF you do double dip, just make sure the woman isn't watching. Or other men for that matter. In fact, don't let the cat catch you.

Eventually you'll get the right balance of oil to vinegar. If the jar is now half full, add more garlic and shallots. If the jar is half-empty, you are a bitter person and need to go find a woman that'll have you, so you can get over it. Tony Soprano saw a therapist; you can too. Pour a little over the salad and mix the salad a bit. If it's tasty, excellent. Add more until it tastes good, or the vinegar rips your face off, whichever comes first. This dressing improves with time, just like this book, so make enough to last a few salads. Just be sure to refrigerate it in between meals or tasty snacks.

A Tasty Variation on the salad:

> Arugula
> Fresh Figs (Green or Mission)
> Cypress Gardens Midnight Moon cheese or other semi-soft gourmet cheese from the deli.

---

[95] More commonly referred to as a "Supermarket." They are designed to lull you into a false sense of happiness so you spend more on cheese.

[96] Or, for real men that used to be real boys, those jars you kept your bugs in.

[97] We don't really need to define this, do we?

[98] A hellofa mess is more than a spill, and less than explosive decompression.

[99] No, not you; shake the jar.

Instead of the living butter lettuce, get some arugula lettuce, quarter some fresh figs, and sprinkle on the Midnight Moon Cheese. Yes, that is really what it is called. No, we don't care if it's a silly name. Do not question our authoritah![100]

Enjoy. The Teutonic Goddess will be with you. Okay, actually she'll be with Jim, but you may land a Teutonic Demi-Goddess.

Caprese Salad

Soundtrack: *That's Amore* by Dean Martin

3 red or yellow vine-ripe Tomatoes, "heirloom"[101] tomatoes preferred

1 pound fresh buffalo mozzarella cheese	Bunch fresh basil
Good extra-virgin olive oil	Good quality balsamic vinegar
Himalayan pink salt	Fresh ground pepper

Using your serrated tomato knife, follow the proper cutting technique (see www.manmeetsstove.com/videoz and click on the "Knife Skillz" video), and slice the tomatoes into ¼-inch thick round slabs. Do the same with the buffalo mozzarella. Yes, yes, we KNOW; the mozzarella might be difficult to find, but man up and GET SOME. It's worth it. If you simply can't work up the cojones to find it, yes, you can use REGULAR mozzarella. We understand; just stop your sniveling. If you really want to step up this salad to pro gourmet, get some fresh burrata cheese instead. If this doesn't get your woman warmed up, it's highly unlikely anything will.

Plate the salad by laying down alternating slices of tomatoes and mozzarella, adding a basil leaf or two between each layer. Alternatively, you can get creative and make tall stacks of tomatoes, basil, and mozzarella on a smaller plate.

Purists would say that a real Caprese salad does not include balsamic vinegar. Well, we say that the purists have got a stick up their nether regions. Balsamic on Caprese salad is like tanning oil on Shakira. Just say "Yes, please."

Bust out a cup of Balsamic vinegar and dump it into a sauce pan big enough to hold it all. Note the starting level of the vinegar. Turn the fire onto high, fire-man,[102] and let the vinegar heat up. When it starts to boil, start whisking it rapidly. Did we say stop? No. Keep whisking until the vinegar is at a level half as high as when you started. Gentlemen, you have just created a "balsamic reduction," and it is GOOD. Taste it, and if you like, you can add just a little bit of sugar to sweeten it up. Yeah. Now pour the reduction back into the vinegar bottle. Yes, go get it out of the recycling bin, and wash it before you use it to store the reduction sauce.

Tip:
No food should go to waste in the kitchen. If in doubt, will it go in a soup?

Drizzle the salad with some olive oil, and some of the Balsamic reduction; season with salt and pepper to taste, and chow down. If you want to impress the ladies, do not pour all of the olive oil and balsamic over the little stacks. Drizzle it around the plate in decorative swirls. If that's too girly for you, it's perfect. You might impress her enough to get some. Don't make us remind you that we know what we are doing.

---

[100] Our apologies to Cartman.
[101] No, this is a species of tomato, NOT a zombie tomato handed down through the family… that would be squishy and gross.
[102] Yes, Torch, we are finally allowing you to turn up the heat!

Soundtrack: One Thing Leads to Another **by The Fixx**

If you were to simply skin some yams, slice them lengthwise and bake, there is nothing wrong with that. But it has been done before, and it tastes… well, it tastes a lot like kissing your aunt.[103] Your taste buds, and hers,[104] deserve a better ride, don't you think? We've been known to call this dish "Screaming Yams of Love." Your mileage may vary. This is a bit of work, but it reheats nicely and it will knock the socks off the in-laws to be, or not to be, depending on your game. Player.

4 yams	Butter	2 eggs
½ cup brown sugar	Pinch or two salt	Splash of vanilla
2 Tablespoons flour		

Preheat the oven to 400 degrees. Wash and then dry them yams, then rub the outsides with butter. Poke the yams a bunch of times with a fork so they don't explode in your oven. Bake the yams in the skin until a fork goes in easy.[105] Should be 45 minutes to 1 hour 15 minutes, depending on how big the yams are.[106] When they are done, the skins will be dark on the outside. Pull them out, and peel 'em. Cut the baked yam up into cubes. Blend the butter, sugar, eggs, salt, vanilla, and flour together in a food processor. You can also use an immersion blender. Add the cubed yams a few at a time and pulse the machine. When the yam mixture is smooth, you are ready for the baking dish.

Lower your oven temperature to 350°. Yep, less heat. Butter up a baking dish and scoop the yam mixture into it. Now for part two:

1 cup brown sugar	⅓ cup flour	Handful of chopped pecans
½ stick butter, softened to room temperature		

Mix together the brown sugar, flour, and nuts, preferably with a mixer if you've got one. Add in the butter and mix until the consistency is even. Toss this mixture on top of the yams. Be generous with both the butter and the pecans; this is not the recipe to skimp on. Remember, you're trying to build up enough resources to draw on for Act 3 later. Bake at 350° for about 30 minutes. Start keeping an eye on it after 20 minutes. You are looking for a nice golden brown color, like a beach bunny towards the end of summer. Those of you that live inland, just use your imagination of what a beach bunny looks like. Those of you that live on the coast? Well done.

---

[103] The one with a mustache.

[104] Your girlfriend, not your 2nd cousin.

[105] This joke was too easy, too.

[106] If you are a cheater, you can put the yams into the microwave for 10 to 20 minutes instead. But as with most things, a slowly-stoked fire brings the best results: resplendent results, lingering results, juicy results.

Polenta Tomato Ring Stack

Soundtrack: *Chiquitita* by ABBA

This is a nice side to go with a spicy Italian sausage.[107] We use this as a side dish, or even a light snack, when we want something and Jody Foster is unavailable. Make sure the basil and tomatoes are as fresh as that young woman you were looking at yesterday.[108] We get ours at the farmers market (good), or our garden (better). The tomatoes and basil, that is, not the young woman.[109]

Avocado	Tomato, "heirloom" preferred
Monterey Jack cheese	Tube of polenta[110]
Flour tortillas	Basil
Salt	Pepper

Using a knife or biscuit cutter, cut disks of tortilla about the same size of the tomatoes you have. Cut enough tortillas to make the number of stacks you want. Plate the tortillas. Slice the cheese, lay it out, and cut it to match your tortilla disks. Set the cheese on the tortilla. Grab the avocado, but this time cut it horizontally to make flat rounds of avocado (to fit within the stack). Some of the slices will have the pit circle in them, and some will not. The avocado rings are easy to peel once you slide them off the pit. Set the avocado rings on top of the cheese rounds.

Set the flames to medium and pour some olive oil into the pan, mince[111] 5 to 10 basil leaves, and toss them into the pan. Slice open the tube of polenta and cut enough rounds for all of your stacks. Set the polenta into the olive oil and heat for 3 to 5 minutes, depending on how thick you sliced them. You want to see a few spots of golden brown on the underside, and then it's time to flip and cook the other side. Set a disk of polenta on top of each growing stack. Sprinkle with freshly ground salt and black pepper between each layer as you stack items up. Place the avocado rounds on next, and then slices of tomato on top of that. Cut some small basil leaves off the twig and stab the stem of the leaf into the tomatoes. Serve with onion rings and quality donuts for a "Triple Ringer."[112]

---

[107] ...or a spicy Italian for that matter.

[108] Pervert.

[109] Pervert.

[110] Pre-made polenta that is wrapped in a plastic tube that looks like a sausage.

[111] Cut into tiny pieces

[112] Don't actually do this unless you are as desperate for a punch line as we were.

Both sides of Thomas's family, back a few generations, have made versions of this simple meal. We present a few of them. True "comfort food" and high in protein. Not as comforting as her running around topless, but pretty comforting nevertheless.[113]

>   2 cups cooked rice (rice cooker preferred; Basmati rice is recommended)
>   4 Tablespoons peanut butter (almost any nut butter will work)[114]

Southern Momma Version

Make some rice using a rice cooker (pro), or boxed instant (rank amateur). Use hot tap water to cream the peanut butter to the consistency of heavy gravy. Pour gravy over the hot rice in a bowl, turn on the TV, and eat your guts out.

Grandpappy's Way

Use hot tap water or milk to cream the peanut butter to the consistency of heavy gravy. You will want to brown 1/2 an onion and 4 garlic cloves in a pan with oil, then mix into the gravy. Pour over the hot rice, eat any excess gravy with a spoon, and enjoy.

Jacquian Path

Nuts (almost anything, except pistachios)	Coconut milk	Red curry paste
Yogurt	Chicken	Rice
Olive oil	Salt and Pepper	Butter

Throw a handful of nuts in the food processor with a little bit of olive oil. Run the food processor in bursts until the nut butter looks creamy. Add a spoonful of red curry paste, and spin some more. Don't bother with dried curry powder. It adds color like a slap to the ass, but is otherwise unrewarding. Pour in coconut milk until it is the consistency of fresh breast milk. See, we could tell you were not paying attention! Actually, add the coconut milk until you get a gravy consistency, or a bit thicker. Taste, and add more curry if it needs more bang, but don't overdo it.[115] If you need some quick protein in a hurry, pour that over rice, add a lump of butter, and eat. Or keep going.

> *Basmati* means "the fragrant one" in Sanskrit.
>
> So does "Chanel" in English.

Thai'd Up Chicken Variation

Pour 2/3 of the gravy into a pitcher or big bowl and set aside. Take the remaining 1/3 of the gravy and add the rest of the can of coconut milk. Run through the food processor or stick blender until well blended. Add a cup of Greek yogurt and blend again. Pour the mixture into a baking dish, place the chicken into the baking dish, and bake at 325° until the chicken is 170° in the thick part (185° if it is a dark meat piece).

Plate some nice Basmati rice, and spoon a few pieces of chicken onto the top of the mound. Warm the gravy in the pitcher, and pour it over the rice and chicken. Drop a few toasted nuts on top, and serve to the missus.

---

[113] If she's bottom-less, why are you still reading this?
[114] Except THAT nut butter…keep that in the sock, buddy.
[115] You might hurt yourself.

Stupid Simple Cranberry Sauce

Soundtrack: *Dreams* by The Cranberries

This is your one trick for the holidays; don't waste it on a work party. Later we can teach you how to pull off the mystery of food-dom, The Thanksgiving Dinner, but for now...this is your game.

We like fruit with our meat; not sure why that is, but it's how we roll. Roasted apples are stuck in the mouth of a whole pig. Pineapple rings go with spiral cut ham. Turkey goes with cranberry sauce like a Brazilian on a sun-tanned, 22 year-old co-ed.[116] Some folk want the jellied cranberry sauce, which is basically canned cranberry Jello.™ You know, so you can cut the cranberry slime into shapes with cookie cutters.[117] We have cousins that heat the canned whole berry cranberry sauce and serve it warm. Whatever the tradition of your family, disregard it at your peril.[118] If your family is open to multiple variations of cranberry sauce, this cranberry sauce is easy to make and hard to screw up, so we thought of you.

¾ cup water

12-ounce bag fresh cranberries[119]

1 cup sugar

¼ teaspoon salt

Bring the water, sugar, and salt to boil in a medium saucepan over high heat, stirring occasionally to dissolve the sugar. Stir in the cranberries, and let the mix return to a boil. Reduce heat to medium, cover, and simmer roughly 5 minutes until the sauce is slightly thickened and about 2/3 of the berries have split open. You will actually hear them popping open like little grenades in your pot, which is half the fun. Pour the sauce into a glass bowl, and let it cool before you serve it. You can make this ahead to save time on the big day, but not more than a week ahead of time. If your relatives eat the canned cranberry snot, you may want to bring a can so you don't cause a family feud. If you are in doubt, bring booze too, assuming they are happy drunks.

---

[116] Just so we know its all legal...

[117] A thrill a minute.

[118] Don't say we didn't warn you. Unless you enjoy starting WWIII at your home. Then, go ahead.

[119] If you can only find frozen cranberries, you will need to add about 2 minutes to the cooking time.

sauces

Pebre

Soundtrack: *Lay it Down* by Journey

Jim was introduced to the joys of Pebre (pronounced pay-bray) when he visited Chile. The family he stayed with set this bowl of green deliciousness in front of him with some fresh baguette bread. Extra crusty bread. Chileans do not screw around with bread. If it was made yesterday, it's trash. Listen to them on that. A word about bread: that white crap your mommy fed you as a child is not bread. That's an edible sponge.

In typical gringo fashion, Jim laid a thick layer of Pebre onto the bread and scarfed it down. The host family all fell on their asses laughing. Apparently, pebre is meant to be scraped onto the bread thin.[120]

Screw that.

FRESH French-style baguette bread	4 bunches fresh cilantro
Mild yellow "Sweet Hungarian" pepper	Red wine vinegar
Olive oil	Himalayan pink salt
Optional: Clove or four of garlic, chopped fine.	Optional: avocado

Fold the cilantro bunches in on themselves until they make a small cigar, instead of a loose bunch of leaves. Cut the cilantro wad extra fine, starting with the top leaves, and when you cut down to mostly stems, stop and throw away the stems. Repeat this method with all four cilantro bunches. Now re-chop them really fine as a pile; see www.manmeetstove.com/videoz and click on the "Knife Skillz" video. Put the cloves of garlic onto the board, and press down on them with the flat of the knife to break them open. Remove the dry skin off the clove and chop the garlic fine. Cut off the stem of the yellow pepper, cut it open lengthwise, and remove the white pulp and seeds.[121] Cut the pepper into strips, and then re-cut the pepper extra fine (minced) as well. Throw these into a bowl with the cilantro and garlic, and add a little red wine, just enough to wet down all the produce. Stir. If it's still too dry, add a little more red wine vinegar, then grind in some salt to taste.

Tear off a hunk of bread off the baguette, and slather the pebre onto the bread. Don't listen to the Chileans. They may know pebre, but we Norte Americanos know excess.

Once you've tried this pebre stuff, you've got to take it over the top. Open the avocado as described in the Guacamole section (page 25), and fork some avocado onto the bread with the pebre. Just squish it all together. Taste that. Yeah. That's right. Now take that over to your lady and feed her some of that action with your fingers. Enjoy.

Cheese Sauce

Soundtrack: *Happy Together* by The Turtles

Cheese was our first word. Okay, it was Thomas'. Jim's was "NOW!" or something similar. Whether yours is mild, sharp, hard, soft, white, yellow, or blue, cheese is just one of the things that makes everything else better when it's around in large quantities, like sex. So it is with cheese sauce, and so it shall be, world without end, amen.

Butter	Flour	Milk
Shredded cheese	Salt, pepper, and chili to taste	

---

[120] Like a sheen of suntan lotion on the side-boob of that 20-something you're not supposed to be ogling.
[121] Or go ahead and leave the seeds in, stud, if you got the nards for their heat.

Melt butter in a saucepan over medium heat. Stir in a little bit of flour, a spoonful at a time, until you have made a paste. What you just did has some fancy French name, but what doesn't? Let the "roux" paste cook, stirring constantly, for about two minutes. The darker it gets, the more flavor you'll have, but the less thick the sauce will be. When it starts to smell a bit like pie crust, you are in the zone. Don't burn it. Slowly add some cold milk, and stir the heck out of it with a wooden spoon as you go. The roux should dissolve into the milk with stirring. Cook over medium-low heat, stirring often, until thickened and just starting to boil: about 10 to 15 minutes. Add the shredded cheese and stir until melted. Taste for seasoning, and add salt, pepper, and chili as desired.

The flavor you get from your cheese sauce can vary greatly with the type of cheese you choose, and the spices. If you have a favorite cheese, try that one. Sharp cheddar is always a favorite.

Jim's Heart Attack Hollandaise

Soundtrack: *Heartbeat of Rock 'n Roll* by Huey Lewis and the News

| 3 Eggs | 1.5 Tablespoons water | 1 stick butter |
| 3 to 4 Tablespoons Tarragon vinegar | Salt and Pepper | |

Start by filling a sink (or a pot larger than the one you will be cooking in) partially with cool water. You'll use this water to rapidly cool the bottom of the cooking pot later.

> **Tip:**
> Do not tell her what is in the Hollandaise.
>
> No, really.

Melt butter in a pot over medium heat (or nuke it until melted). Completely melt the butter, but not so it's burning hot. Crack open the eggs and place them into a bowl. Add water to the bowl and whisk the eggs and water together very well, until they are one color throughout.

Now comes the hard part. Turn the heat down on the butter pot. If you look at the flame, you want it to be a 2 on a 5 scale: the 5 being full flame; the 1 being almost no flame. Use "Low" heat, but not too low. If not sure, go lower, not hotter, until you get the hang of it. Lower heat will simply take a little longer, and your whisk arm may fall off. If you go too hot, the eggs will become little scrambled bits in a butter mix, not a sauce. You can recover this by blending the hell out of it.[122]

Pour the egg mixture into the melted butter, and start whisking gently (go faster if you see visible egg bits starting to float around in your pot). **Do not stop whisking.** The goal is to keep the eggs from forming a thin omelet on the bottom of the pot. You want to keep stirring until the eggs "go off," and thicken the mixture from a liquid to a gravy-like sauce. When you see it turning into the desired thickness of a sauce, immediately pull the pot off the fire, and put the pot bottom into the cold water in the sink. This ensures that the bottom of the pot is immediately cooled off, and stops cooking the sauce. You may want to keep whisking for a little bit longer while it cools down a bit.

Now here's the thing - we are told that people use lemon for Hollandaise sauce. Why? We have no idea. It tastes a bit like dessert that way. We like tarragon

---

[122] Your clergy will thank you.

vinegar, and like it much. Once you cool the pot a little, take it out, add two tablespoons of vinegar, and taste the sauce. If it is strong enough for you, excellent. We usually add at least two more tablespoons of tarragon vinegar, or more, to taste. Sometimes we make it light for our guests, and "rip-your-face-off" strong for ourselves, in a separate small pitcher.

Salt and pepper to taste.

Sometimes people use just the egg yolks in the sauce. The sauce will be really thick and tasty if you do it that way.[123]

Now all of this involved process, we are told, can be avoided by the use of a double boiler to even the heat out and cook the sauce slowly, but that is cheating and we will not give you you're Girl Scout chef merit badge if you do it. Actually, we have never had a double boiler when we needed it, and see them as somewhat of a unitasker (bad), unless one makes candy a lot.

You can also do a similar process in a blender, or a microwave. Or both. How embarrassing. Half the fun of this recipe is making it like a pro.

We generally make 2 to 3 times this recipe, and eat it on broccoli cooked al dente. Please do NOT overcook the broccoli, American style. Limp broccoli is a vile abomination unto the gods.

Thomas' Barbeque Sauce

Soundtrack: *Sweet Dreams (Are Made Of This)* **by Beyonce**

There are those who rub sauce on their meat,[124] and those who don't. If you are a sauce-r, then read on. If you are a dry rub-ber,[125] then you can skip to the Melange BBQ Rub (page 50). Or you can do BOTH. The job of the sauce is to bring the meat to a different land of flavor. You could think of it as a happyland for your meat.[126] The basic sauce is only a starting point. As you should have figured out by now, we play with our food. There are endless things to learn about the chemistry between fat, the other liquids, and the semi-solids. Yeah, we just saw you nodding off. Moving on...

Olive oil   Vinegar

Fat (Thomas' choice is bacon fat, but use what you want)
Tomato products (tomato sauce, enchilada sauce, ketchup, paste, juice, or actual tomatoes)
Some form of sugar (brown sugar, white sugar, or turbinado sugar)
Liquid sugar (honey, molasses, maple syrup, or agave syrup)
Citrus juice (lemon, lime, orange, grapefruit, or kumquat)

Spices: garlic, onion, leeks, chives, shallots, radishes, peppers (BRING IT, DUDE), bay, oregano, basil, thyme, mustard, paprika, chili powder, and on and on. If it smells good, chop it fine and stir it in. Don't get too far ahead with the flavors, though, minute man. Taste the sauce as you go so you don't overdo it.

Start with two big glugs of olive oil in a glass bowl. What is a glug, you ask? About 1/4 cup. Add about half that much bacon fat (1/4 cup, or about what you get from eight strips of bacon), and give it a splash of the best wine

---

[123] Screw your cholesterol. This is cooking.
[124] Who are we to judge?
[125] ...ouch!
[126] The Playboy mansion being the other one.

vinegar you have, then stir it up. Look at how much is in the bowl, and double that by adding tomato products (tomato juice, tomato paste, ketchup, enchilada sauce, and/or fresh tomatoes). Stir again. If it is still too close to toothpaste in thickness, add a splash more tomato juice and a capful of the vinegar, and stir it up again. Get it to a liquid state that reminds you of a thick, rich soup. Now add two finger pinches of brown sugar, and two good, long squeezes of a liquid sugar. Stir that all up, and set aside. Okay, go ahead and taste it.[127] That is the base that you will add flavors to. If it is too sweet, then don't squeeze your honey so dang hard, and add more tomato and vinegar.

Take all the fresh stuff (produce and herbs) that you are going to use, and mince them up small. Pour a splash of olive oil into your frying pan, and add all of the peppers and onion and other produce, roughly two finger pinches of each. Heat that over medium until it all starts to smell good, and the onions, peppers, and garlic are soft. Don't burn them; pay attention as you cook here. Remember that your woman is watching (if you let her), and when she sees that you don't have the attention span long enough to avoid burning these, she is going to know that you only have the attention span to cover your 30 seconds of pleasure in bed, will leave her wanting more, and she will be forced to dump you and become a lesbian. Patience. Good things come to those who cook.

Add the sauce from the bowl to the pan, and toss in whatever other spices you are going to use. Don't forget some freshly ground black pepper. Heat on low until it smells like you want to stick your face in there[128] and drink it, or for about five minutes. Add ¼ cup fresh citrus, pour it into a blender and whizz it up, or use a stick blender.

Saucy.

Diagnosis: if it is too spicy for you, send it to us. Next time, don't put so many peppers in, or lower the Scofield heat index on the ones that you do add. If it is too runny, then add more solids, or less of the really wet stuff.[129] If it is far too good, and you end up drinking it out of a big mug with a fat curlicue straw while you watch TV, then you need to get out more often, but you got the sauce right.

Pasta Sauce Three Way

Soundtrack: *Hey Mickey* by Toni Basil

Quick and Dirty[130]

Okay 008, this is a tricky mission, and it is going to require special skills. Before she gets to your house, buy the best looking jar of pasta sauce you can find, *or afford;* a pack of pre-sliced mushrooms; and one each of those toothpaste-looking tubes of garlic, peppers, tomato paste, and basil. If you manage to find your way home, get out the 2-quart sauce pan, and pour in the jar of pasta sauce.[131] Run the tap water until hot, and put ½-cup of hot water in the jar, close with the lid on, and shake.[132] Pour the red water into the sauce pan as well. Open the pack of mushrooms and empty into the sauce. Add a squeeze from each of the tubes. The tomato paste should get a good, big, long squeeze, and the other three should get shorter squeezes (smaller amounts). Give it a stir. Put the tubes in the fridge and put the sauce jar out in the trash, or better yet, in someone else's trash. Heat the sauce up low and slow; you just want her to simmer.[133] The sauce should warm up as well. Stir often so it doesn't stick to

---

[127] Use a clean spoon, not your fingers; do not double-dip, and wash your hands, you slob!

[128] This is certain to make you popular in other ways.

[129] Really wet is great to find in a woman; not so great in barbeque sauce.

[130] Yeah, we know that's how you like it.

[131] Don't spatter yourself. She isn't there, sport.

[132] ...her all night long.

[133] True of many things.

the bottom.[134] Don't go claiming that you MADE this sauce; just serve it on some nice al dente pasta and change the subject.

Fresh and Nimble

You want easy? Well, who doesn't? This is also easy and quick, and in this case both are good. This Quick and Dirty Sauce is full of flavor even though it is mostly from a can.

Big can of tomatoes (Italian diced San Marzano are best)	Italian tomato paste
White button mushrooms	1 onion
4 garlic cloves	Basil and oregano
Fresh tomatoes[135] (farmer's market "heirloom" are best)	Butter

When selecting mushrooms, they should be bright, white, and pretty off the rack.[136] If they look brown, bruised, and beaten, pass on to the next stall. Bust out a 2-quart or larger sauce pan and a frying pan. Start the frying pan on medium, drop in a tablespoon or two of butter, dice the garlic and onion (see www.manmeetsstove.com/videoz and click on the "Knife Skillz" video), and stir with a wooden spoon. When it starts to smell really good, add in the mushrooms. You can chop the 'shrooms, slice them, or leave them whole, depending on the texture of sauce you want. Rein in the flames to low, cowboy, and wait out the 'shrooms. They will shrink up like you on a day at the lake in February.[137] As soon as the mushrooms have shed their excess water, you are ready to mix it up. Open up the cans and dump the tomatoes into the cold sauce pan. Kill the fire under the frying pan, and spoon all that buttery mushroom goodness into the sauce pan on top of the tomatoes. Set the fire to low under the sauce pan. Give it a stir every few minutes. Dice the fresh tomatoes. Add the diced fresh tomatoes into the pot, and stir. When it is all heated up, add in the basil and oregano to taste, and serve. The longer you let the sauce sit, the bigger the flavor, so you can also fridge it[138] and serve tomorrow for dinner on some pasta.

Playboy Perfect

To bring your sauce into the realm of art...

Farm fresh tomatoes, "heirloom" preferred	Sweet or hot Italian sausage
White button mushrooms	Portobello mushroom
Porcini mushroom	Chicken stock
Onion	Garlic
Zucchini squash	Basil and oregano
Butter	Olive oil

---

[134] That's what SHE said.

[135] Two, if they are well-rounded and firm, like any good pair.

[136] We think all racks should have a bright and ready look to them.

[137] Shrinkage does happen.

[138] Not frigid; that would be your ex, but that is probably your fault because you didn't have this book to save your ass.

If your chicken stock is frozen because you made it yourself,[139] then pull some out of the freezer and drop it into the big sauce pan and let it sit there. If you have bought some chicken stock, pour half the container in the pan, and save the rest for some other adventure.

Get the grill going, and paint the sausage and the Portobello 'shroom with garlic butter.[140] Grill the sausage on one side, and when you flip it, put the 'shroom on the top rack. When cooked through and smelling good, pull the sausage[141] and 'shroom steak off the grill, and dice them up into bite-sized chunks. Don't burn your piggies.[142] Put the chunks aside for the moment. If you eat all the sausage now, the sauce is going to be a bit flat, so knock it off; smart cooks grill up another sausage for themselves to munch on while working.[143]

Start heating the diced onion and minced garlic in the frying pan with our good friend, butter. The more the merrier, as the butter actually helps develop the final sauce flavor and texture. When the onion starts to turn a bit clear, add in the two raw bunches of mushrooms. Shrink the 'shrooms down, then kill the heat.

Put the sausage and portabellas into the pot, but hold back two sausage chunks. Chop the saved sausage chunks up really small (minced), and put 'em into the pot. Add the contents of the frying pan, and stir. Start the heat on low. Slow heat wins the game here, which is true of most things Italian, or female, or Italian females. Dice the tomatoes, making sure to catch the juice. Add all the tomato bits (except the stem end) and juice into the mix. Mince the zucchini into tiny bits, and dump it into the sauce. Add in the oregano and basil, tasting as you go; bring the whole thing up to temperature, and then kill the heat. Store your masterpiece[144] sauce in the fridge for a day, and then heat to serve.

---

[139] Stud

[140] Garlic butter: mince (cut really fine) five cloves of garlic, and mix with half a stick of melted butter. Refrigerate until used.

[141] No, not your sausage. Try to stay focused here.

[142] Sausage OR fingers.

[143] Save your sausage for her later, though.

[144] Yeah, this may well get you a piece.

booze and beverages

Be wary of strong drink. It can make you shoot at tax collectors...and miss. – Robert A. Heinlein

It was recently determined by scientists that Americans drink less than any other developed nation on earth. Jim thinks this is an area of American underachievement that we can help you correct! Jim always says that there is real alcohol - such as whiskey, gin, vodka, and tequila - and then there is everything else. Beer hasn't been processed through a still enough times to be a real drink. But, Jim understands, some men need longer to fully come into their own than others.

Bloody Mary Classica

Soundtrack: *In my House* by the Mary Jane Girls

So you tied one on big time last night, and now you're really hurtin'. Well, it may not be noon in Peoria, or wherever you are, but it is NOW, capiche? This classic Bloody Mary should help with that hair-of-the-dog.[145]

2 oz. vodka	3 oz. tomato juice	Juice of ½ of a squeezed lemon
3 dashes Worcestershire sauce	2 drops Tabasco sauce	Cracked black pepper
Freshly ground salt		

Shake all the ingredients in a shaker with ice, and strain into a chilled highball glass over crushed ice. If you don't know what a highball glass is, use a large mug. Stick in a lemon wedge and a celery stalk. Drink up, and feel the love.

Now if you want to experiment, and who doesn't, here are a few ways to mix it up. You can use sake, scotch, or gin, but back off the booze by a ½ ounce. You can add about 6 capers, or use lime instead of lemon. Add a little clam juice,[146] or use a different hot sauce instead of Tabasco; just be sure not to blow yourself away. Lastly, a little horseradish can really kick Mary up a notch. Just don't do all of these things at once! Trial and error. If you get too much of something in your glass that doesn't work, add more tomato, vodka, or maybe a little lemon to tang it out. Dilution is the solution.

If you have time to prepare in advance, you can take the tomato juice, Worcestershire, and Tabasco sauce, mix, and pour into an ice cube tray. Freeze overnight and use for the ice. That way there is minimal dilution of the blessed booze.

Apple Pie – The Drink

Soundtrack: *American Pie* by Don McLean

Unfiltered Apple Cider	Rum
Cinnamon sticks	Sugar

The first time Jim made a batch of Apple Pie, he opened the bottle of cider, poured all the cider into a big bowl, and added the sugar and rum to taste. Stirred it well until the sugar had dissolved, threw the cinnamon sticks into the former cider jar, poured the mixture back into the jar, recapped it, and stuck it up into the cupboard and forgot about it. He drank (slowly) what wouldn't fit back in the jar. About a year later, he was getting ready to move, and guess what he found hidden up in the cupboard? Yeah, heaven in a bottle. The bottle cap vacuum seal

---

[145] If it isn't helping, you're doing it wrong.
[146] Get away from her! That is NOT the clam juice we were referring to.

actually *popped* again, which Jim assumes was due to some of the sugar and cider converting to alcohol. Whatever it was, that Apple Pie was smooooooth and delicious.   Go ye therefore and do likewise.

If you must drink it on the spot though, we understand. Self-control isn't for everyone.

Limoncello

Soundtrack: *The Lemon Song* by Led Zeppelin

NOTICE: Takes 5 days. Patience, worm! Good stuff requires TIME to be truly delicious.

12 lemons	One 750-ml bottle of Vodka or Everclear
2½ cups sugar	3½ cups water
Bottles	

Italians make some pretty good stuff. This includes, but is not limited to: fast cars, Italian women (fast optional), pasta, sausages, and of course, booze. Limoncello is amongst their finest, right after the women.

This is going to require either a microplane, or a cheese grater on the fine side. You can also use a vegetable peeler or paring knife, but it will be a real nuisance/ headache/time consumer. Take a lemon and zest[147] the skin of the entire lemon into a bowl. The trick is to get all the good yellow part of the skin peels, and none of the bitter white "pith" beneath the lemon skin. If you get very much white pith into the bowl, trim it off the skin, and trash it. Pith on it. Zest all 12 lemons, and set the zest aside.

> A microplane is a woodshop tool that was adapted to the kitchen so well that they now outsell the woodworking tool. Use it to finely grate cheese, spices like whole nutmeg, or to make limoncello!

Get a glass 1 gallon container, preferably with a lid. Put the zest/peels into the container and pour the bottle of hooch (vodka) over it. Cover with the lid or plastic wrap, and let the liquid mixture steep for four days on the kitchen counter.

On day four, put the water and sugar into a saucepan and heat until the sugar dissolves. Let it cool down, and then pour the sugar mixture (which bartenders call "simple syrup") in with the vodka and lemon zest mixture. Cover and let the mixture set for one more day. Bust out either a big bottle, or a lot of small bottles, and pour the

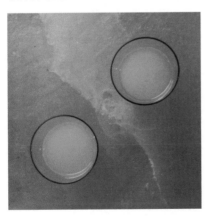

limoncello into the bottles through a strainer to catch the lemon peels as the liquid goes through. If you do not have a strainer, use a CLEAN cheesecloth draped over the bottle, but pour VERY slowly, or you'll spray sticky liquid all over your kitchen. Probably not the first time you did that, but that was hopefully not in the kitchen...[148]

Once you have successfully transferred the limoncello to bottles, seal them up and refrigerate. It should keep for a month.

Fire up the Godfather, serve her a meal of pasta with one of our fine sauces, and pour her the limoncello in a shot glass after the meal. This stuff is potent. Hopefully so are you.

Variations: use oranges, limes, grapefruit, or a mixture of the above for more hootch-y fun.

---

[147] Zest = finely grate using the tool you have. No not that tool, the microplane or grater.
[148] If it was, well done. Now disinfect that kitchen. With soap.

Mistress Margarita

Soundtrack: *Lady Marmalade* by Christina Aguilera

Ice
One shot freshly squeezed lime juice
Salt (optional)

Two shots 100 percent agave tequila
½ shot Cointreau (Triple Sec, if you must)
Sugar (1 teaspoon or to taste)

Grab two large tumblers or frosty mugs that had been previously placed in the freezer. If you are going to use salt (and what pinhead wouldn't?), pour the salt into a flat dish to make a nice layer, wet the rim of the glass with a wet paper towel, and dip the rim of the glass into the dish of salt. The rim should be covered with salt.

Fill the mug with ice, and throw in the booze. Add a little sugar (to taste). Stir with your finger. Lick finger. Okay, that's your drink. For hers, use a spoon, at least if she is watching. Or use HER finger, then lick that. Viva Mexico!

Cosmopolitan

Soundtrack: *Sex and the City Theme Song* by the Pfeifer Broz. Orchestra

We certainly hope you are making this at the request of a woman dressed in less clothes than a swimsuit model. Any man that has read this far into the book should have a pair of big swingin' brass ones and a taste for much more macho drinks than this. A shot of whiskey with a human hair in it, for example. However, in the pursuit of the feminine, we understand. By all means proceed...

Ice
1 shot cranberry juice

2 shots vodka
Long thin piece of orange peel curl

1 shot Cointreau

1 shot Rose's lime juice or 2 teaspoons fresh squeezed lime juice

Chill two cocktail glasses in the freezer. Cocktail glasses are the ones that James Bond uses for his martinis. Combine the ingredients over cracked ice, and strain the liquids into the chilled glasses.

To make the orange curl, take a well-washed and scrubbed orange, and with a sharp paring knife cut a long, wide strip of peel off the orange as you spin the orange in your hand. Carefully! Flatten the peel out on the cutting board and, using your big chef's knife, cut or scrape away any remaining white pithy crap off the inside of the orange peel. Pith is not very tasty. It tastes like pith. Cut the orange peel into very thin strips. They should curl up as you cut them. Hang a curl on the edge of the martini glass like your toes on the edge of a surfboard, and serve to the lady. Even if the drink is as foofy as a pink poodle, if she likes it, well, who are we to judge you if you give her every inch of what she wants?

Vodka Martini, Shaken not….

Soundtrack: *Live and Let Die* by Guns N' Roses

If your car has an oil slick that isn't coming from the engine compartment, an ejection seat, and is made in Great Britain… If you have an unnatural desire to wear a custom-fit of suit so you can hide your shoulder-holstered Walther PPK… If you find yourself wanting to refer to your boss by a single letter of the alphabet… If you like bedding bad girls while catching bad guys, you probably will also want to know how to make the "real" spy martini.

The regulation Spy Martini is as follows:

Three shots of Gordon's Gin
½ shot of Kina Lillet

One shot of vodka
Slice of lemon-peel

Place the booze into a shaker with ice and shake until ice-cold. Throw in the lemon peel.

Here's the problem. Kina Lillet apparently no longer exists. There is a Lillet Blanc, but it is fruitier than Kina Lillet. Ah well. Here's our modern version:

1 VERY chilled Martini glass
1 shot Vodka
1 drop Angostura Bitters
Slice of Lemon peel

3 Shots Gordon's Gin
½ shot of Lillet Blanc
Ice

Take the glass tumbler, fill it with the drink ingredients, and add ice until covered. Cap tumbler with cocktail shaker and shake vigorously for about three seconds. Strain the alcohol into the chilled martini glass, and add the slice of lemon peel. Drink up. Keep that pinkie finger DOWN while you drink it, stud.

Rock this - you just had a weak martini. The shaking actually adds little bits of ice to the drink and waters it down as it melts. If you want to be MORE studly than Her Majesty's Service, stir your martini.

Yeah, we said it, British spies are lightweights. Deal with it.

No Pickup Line Needed

Soundtrack: *Sex and Candy* by Marci Playground

We aren't gonna lie to you, this is another stone-cold-simple chick drink. If anyone sees you drinking it, just claim you were testing it to make sure the secret pheromones you mixed in are at the right concentration to get her clothes off.

Vermeer Dutch chocolate liqueur
Ghirardelli Chocolate Black Label chocolate sauce

Bailey's® Irish cream

Mix equal parts of each liquid in a tall glass. If it is hot out, put in all in a blender with two scoops of vanilla ice cream, and mix. Or, you can make it hot inside, and drink it afterwards.

Malted Make Out

Soundtrack: *Your Body is a Wonderland* by John Meyer

You know that her mouth is hot, and we know you think about it all the time. So, make her something sweet, cool, and chocolate-y. This dessert drink is frothy, chilled goodness. You will need a few tall, thick glasses. Put them in the freezer now; you will need them chilled at the end of this run.

Gear up the blender. If you have a smoothie-making blade, we won't tell anyone, but this is the ONE time when you might actually need it. Put the whole thing in the freezer to chill it down. Set a cereal-sized bowl in the freezer as well.

Best chocolate ice cream you can find	Best chocolate syrup you can find
Heavy whipping cream	Malted milk powder
Fluff or marshmallow cream	Cinnamon
Nutmeg	Optional: Chocolate or Coffee liqueur

Get the ice cream home, and in the freezer fast. Put the heavy whipping cream in there, too. Use a tablespoon to scoop out four spoonfuls of marshmallow cream, fold them up in wax paper, and set them in the freezer; they will firm up in there, and take the place that might be frozen banana in a more traditional malt.

Set out the ice cream scoop, your $1/4$, $1/2$, and $2/3$ measuring cups, and a clean tablespoon. Put three scoops of ice cream into the bowl, and then get the bowl back in the freezer.

The difference between a nice, chilled chocolate drink and an average drink is that this is a speed run, and the colder it all is, the better. So work fast; don't worry too much about exact quantities, bang it together, blend it, and serve it.

Mount the blender[149] (not *that* kind of mount – we mean put the pitcher part on the motor part, you crazy freak). Pour in $2/3$ cup of cream, $1/4$ cup of chocolate syrup, a heaping tablespoon of malted milk powder, and three of the frozen marshmallow blobs. Put the lid on the blender, and hit that button. Occasionally the blender will want to clog up because it is too cold. Just shake it a bit to get it going. When the drink is properly smooooooth and frothy, add in the ice cream a little at a time, and blend until it's smooth again. Here's where you can add the optional chocolate or coffee liqueur, then a little more ice cream, and blend 'til smooth. Pour this deliciousness into the frozen glasses. Sprinkle a little bit of nutmeg and cinnamon on top, and dress it up with a chocolate stick or a mint leaf. Abandon the mess you just made, pick up the two glasses, walk out and give one to her. Later, slightly warm up the leftover bottle of chocolate syrup in some warm water. You know where to paint tit.

---

[149] Get off of the counter; mounting the blender means putting the glass part on the motor.

Atomic Lime Spheres

Soundtrack: *She Blinded Me with Science* by Thomas Dolby

Yes, we know that you can't drink these, but these little atomic numbers are what Jello™ shots want to be when they grow up. Be careful with them; they will make you stupid.[150]

Box of Nilla wafers	Package of lime frozen concentrate
Cryptonic Lemon Lime Liqueur	

Yeah, we think Nilla Wafer is a dumbass name, too. Get 'em anyway. Leave the frozen stuff out on the counter when you know you are going to make these. Bust out the blender, dump in about half the box of cookies, and run the machine until you have cookie crumbs. Pour in a splash of the lime concentrate and then run the blender, then pour in a splash of the Cryptonic, and blend again. Now open it up and taste. Since you are not going anywhere after you eat these, you have plenty of time to get them right. Keep adding the two liquids until you have a thick mixture. If you make a dent in it with the spoon, the dent should stay there and not run back. If the mixture is too wet, add more cookie crumbs.

If you don't have a blender, you can take the bag of Nilla's out of the box, and beat the hell out of them in the bag. When the bag explodes and wafer dust settles over your house like a Saudi sand storm, you know you've gone too far. Don't breathe that shit, it'll kill you. Kidding, mostly. Open the bag and mix in the liquids as described above, only kneading[151] the bag to mix it.

You can take out spoonfuls of the mixture and roll them into balls, or flatten them out into little disks. Either way, the next step is up to you. You can roll them in a bowl of powdered sugar, dip them in chocolate, or roll them in coconut. Chill, then serve cold.

Remember to operate machinery with caution after you have taste-tested any of these. In fact, stay away from the machinery. Put the Hummer away.

---

[150] Well… MORE stupid…Hmm… Maybe they will make HER stupid and she'll be, shall we say, more inclined to stay. Nah.
[151] That massaging thing you want to do with her breasts. Only harder.

dessert

Spicy Bacon Candy

Soundtrack: *Candy Man* by Christina Aguilera

Bacon is all the rage right now. Bacon Vodka. Bacon Chocolate Bars. Yeah, we get it; bacon is like the gods' way of showing us they love men. That, and redheads that match on both ends.

So how does one improve upon the best food on earth? This is why you are hanging with us. Add hot pepper. Yeah.

Bacon, thick or thin cut.   Brown sugar   Chili Flakes

Pre-heat oven to 350 degrees. Get a clean plastic bag, and pour in a little brown sugar in the bottom. Drop the bacon into the plastic bag with the brown sugar.   Close the bag, and shake until the pig is thoroughly coated in brown sugar. Open bag, repeat with more pork.

Line a baking sheet with aluminum foil to allow for grease drainage. Crinkle the aluminum foil as you lay it in the baking sheet so that there are hills and valleys to lay the bacon on. The idea is to have the bacon sit upon the ridges, and fat and oil to drain into the valleys. The other way is to get a grill/rack to put on top of the aluminum foil. You want to make sure that the air circulates around the bacon and that the fat drains off. Lay out the bacon on the aluminum foil, making sure not to overlap bacon pieces.

Bust out the chili pepper flakes. If you're a girlie-man, you can skip this step. If you like to eat spicy food until you can't sit down the next day, you're one of us. Sprinkle some pepper flakes onto the top of the bacon strips. Use your sphincter judgment as to how much is too hot for you. If some pepper flakes miss the bacon strips and fall into the tray, no big deal.

> Sugar doesn't melt.
>
> It decomposes.
>
> Like a ZOMBIE.

Bake until the bacon is crispy. Remove the tray from the oven, and using tongs (Caution: VERY hot), place the bacon strips onto paper towels to cool and harden before serving.

Break the dried pieces, when cool, into 1-inch squares, or break them into much smaller pieces of bacon candy to use as a garnish (add-on) to salads, especially spinach salad. It also makes a kick-ass ice cream topping.

Now for the *real* fun. Melt some good semi-sweet or bittersweet chocolate in a pot, and when melted, stir in the candied bacon pieces that you have not already eaten. Spoon the chocolate porcine mixture out into little blobs onto some wax paper. Allow to cool. Now you have little bits of heaven, hell, and bacon. Enjoy.

Soundtrack: *High in the Morning* by Tom Petty and the Heart Breakers

As your mentors, we think that you should have mastered the art of making four kinds of cookies as part of your bid to take over the kitchen: a chocolate chip cookie, a peanut butter cookie, a butterscotch cookie, and a "wild one" cookie. Each one will have a few unique ingredients that will go into it; however, they all have the same basic gear recommendations. We recommend two edgeless, non-stick, air-bake cookie sheets; a rack;[152] a cookie scoop; and a plastic spatula. If you don't have all the gear, you can make do with cookie sheets and a spoon.

The cookie sheets and spatula can be easily obtained from most grocery stores with a cooking aisle. The rack and scoop can be found in well-stocked grocery stores, or a cooking store, or online.

Chocolate Chip Cookies

When you say Elvis is King, no one asks "of what?" Likewise, Nestle has a GREAT cookie recipe called Toll House Cookies,™ and it is a universally recognized superb starting point. However, Thomas had a few adjustments, naturally:

2½ cups all-purpose flour	1 teaspoon baking soda	1 teaspoon salt
1 cup (2 sticks) butter, softened	1½ cups packed brown sugar	1 teaspoon vanilla extract
2 large eggs	A few shakes of cinnamon	1 cup chopped nuts
2 cups (12-oz. pkg.) chocolate chips		

Preheat your hotbox[153] to 375°. Put the flour, baking soda, and salt into a small to medium-sized bowl. Toss them really well, so that the baking soda and salt is distributed evenly. Mix the butter, brown sugar, and vanilla in a large bowl until creamy and thoroughly mixed. Jim has his Grandma's regulation Bauer™ cookie bowl that is 12 inches in diameter, and about 80 years old.[154] Add in the eggs, one at a time, beating the mixture together well after adding each egg. Pour in the flour mixture slowly, a little at a time. Stir in the chocolate chips and nuts.

Bring the cookie scoop into action, scooping little bits of cookie dough (about a tablespoon each), and placing them on the cookie sheets to make rows of uniform-sized cookies. If they are all the same size, then they will all bake the same. Bake for 9 to 11 minutes, or until the cookies appear golden brown and tasty. Let the cookies cool on the baking sheets for a couple of minutes, and then place them on the racks to finish cooling.

Peanut Butter Cookies

½ cup butter	¾ cup creamy peanut butter	1¼ cups brown sugar, packed
3 tablespoons cream	Splash of vanilla	Egg
1¾ cups flour	¾ teaspoon salt	¾ teaspoon baking soda

---

[152] Yes, we know how you like a good rack.

[153] No, not her hotbox, the oven. Although you can warm up her hotbox while you wait for the oven to heat.

[154] Yes, he's bragging. Deal with it.

Preheat oven to 375°. Melt the butter in a pan, and cook off some of the water without burning the butter. In a big bowl, add the butter, peanut butter, sugar, cream, and the splash of vanilla. Mix well, and then add the egg. Mix some more. In a separate bowl, mix the flour, salt, and soda. Add the dry stuff into the wet stuff, and mix them until just combined. If you're doing it right, your mixing arm should have fallen off by now.

Use the scoop first, and then flatten the round balls into discs. For some reason, the international symbol that says "peanut butter cookies" is a crossed-fork pattern pressed into the cookie to make a grid. It won't change the flavor, but if you don't do it, someone will ask you, "What kind of cookies are these?" You could start an international incident from your kitchen. We wouldn't want that.[155]

Bake cookies for 8 minutes. Yank them out a bit early if you like Chewbacca peanut cookies;[156] if you like Count Crunch-A-Lot, bake them into the danger zone of 8 minutes and 20 seconds. Cool on the racks. If you are really trying to impress her, half-dip the cookies in melted chocolate once they cool down.

Cake Mix Scotch and Butter Cookies

Chocolate cake mix	½ cup butter
Bag of butterscotch chips	2 eggs

Melt the butter over medium heat in a pan, but do NOT burn the butter. We just want you to cook off some of the water that is in the butter. Dump the cake mix into a big bowl, crack in the eggs, pour the melted butter in, and mix it all up. Now add the bag of butterscotch chips.

Chips, whether chocolate or butterscotch, have a serious role to play in the cookie. Cookies are really a melted chip delivery system. So to make sure you have enough of them, keep adding chips until they don't seem to mix in anymore. There should be a handful of chips in the bowl with bits of dough stuck on them for you to eat when you are done.[157] Preheat the oven to 350°.

Bring the cookie scoop into action, scooping little bits of cookie dough (about a tablespoon each), and placing them on the cookie sheets to make rows of uniform-sized cookies. Bake the cookies for about 10 minutes, but you need to JUST STAND THERE and watch them bake. Think of it as a Kung Fu exercise. Practice your Crane Kick while you wait, or something. The reason you are watching the cookies is that oven temperatures and bake times vary. Pull the cookie sheets out at six minutes and give them a jiggle, and then every couple of minutes after that, and repeat. When they're done, the center of the cookie should be firm,[158] not jiggly like jam or jelly.[159]

You will put one sheet of cookies in the middle of the oven, let them bake, pull them out, and slide the other sheet in. Let the new, hot ones cool a bit; then, using the spatula, transfer them onto the cooling rack. Set the cookie sheet in the sink at an angle, and scrape any remaining cookie footprints off with the spatula. Now you are ready to scoop again. Repeat until you have baked or eaten all the raw dough.

---

[155] Or would we? *Places pinkie finger near mouth*
[156] "chewy"
[157] See? We are just thinking of you and your needs.
[158] Like your teenage self looking at Kate Upton. Or your 40-something self for that matter.
[159] Or breasts. Just sayin'.

Pumpkin Chocolate Chip Cookies (e.g., your Wild Card)

These cookies are a very "Winter Holiday Party in Your Mouth," so they are good to make when that time of year rolls round. They are a bit challenging, but even the failures will be good eating, so give them a practice run or two.

½ cup butter	1 cup brown sugar, packed	1 egg
1 cup canned pumpkin	Splash vanilla	2 cups flour
1 Tablespoon baking powder	1 Tablespoon baking soda	Cinnamon
Nutmeg	1 Tablespoon salt	

Chocolate chips (enough 'til they fall out of the dough)

Preheat oven to 350°. Melt the butter and cook off some of the water, but don't burn it! Mix butter and brown sugar until fluffy. Add egg, pumpkin, and vanilla. You may want a mixer for this one.

In a separate bowl, combine all the dry stuff, and mix it well with a small whisk. Add the dry stuff to the wet stuff in the mixer, and then mix until it is well combined. Stir in the chocolate chips. This dough will be very soft. Bring on the scoop and the cookie sheets and get to work. Bake 10 to 12 minutes, and then cool them on the rack.

Go get yourself invited to a party, preferably with LOTS of women. Pass out the cookies. Oh, come on, if you are married then you are the one guy in the room who is obviously there because of how well he spoils his wife. On the other hand, if you are single… well, my young friend, it is a room full of women. Get phone numbers. Carefully.

Peppermint Pat-Her-Fannies

Soundtrack: *If You Want to Touch Her, ASK!* by Shania Twain

Want to pat her fanny, but don't have exclusive rights to do so yet? Next time don't buy chocolates…make her homemade peppermint patties.

Half block of cream cheese	Bag of powdered sugar	Mint oil

Bag of good chocolate chips (Ghirardelli, minimum)
Optional: peppermint hard candy

Put the cream cheese in a glass bowl, pour in some sugar, and stir it in. This will take a bit of work; at first it will seem like it is not mixing, but as it warms up, all of a sudden it will blend. Add more sugar and mix it in. Taste. If it tastes mostly like cheese, add more sugar, and mix it in. Taste. Keep going until it tastes good.

When it finally tastes like sweet creamy goodness, open the mint oil, and take a whiff. Smell that minty goodness? Pour a bit into the cream cheese and sugar mixture, stir it in, and then taste it. Repeat until the mint pops in your mouth and the cream cheese melts right after it.

Extra Point Pro-tip: Clean and cover the business end of a hammer with plastic wrap, and hold the plastic in place with a rubber band. Find some peppermint hard candy and bash it up with a hammer. Do NOT do this on your very expensive kitchen counter. Stir the broken bits of candy into the cream cheese mixture.

Cover the bowl of the cream filling and place in the fridge.

Meanwhile, in the man cave: Pour the chocolate into a large measuring cup or bowl. Heat the chocolate in the nuke for 30 seconds; stir, and repeat; stirring each time until most, or all, of the chocolate chips are melted. Stir steady now until it is smooth and shiny. If it is not smooth and shiny, you overheated it; but you may be able to save it. Maybe. Quickly pour it into a cool bowl, and add another handful or two of chocolate chips, and stir. If you get back to the shiny place, you are good to go. If not, you have wasted even more chocolate, and you must throw it away and start over. No, we aren't laughing.

Pull the bowl of filling out of the fridge, open it up, taste it again,[160] scoop up a spoonful, and roll it into a little ball with your hands. You did wash those paws thoroughly with soap and water first, right? Gently press it into a little patty and drop it into the chocolate. Roll it around in the chocolate, and then fish it out with a salad fork. Really...it's the short fork with the wide tines. Okay, just look it up on Wikipedia. Use a paring knife to slide the patty out onto the wax paper. Repeat until all the patties are coated in delicious chocolate. When they're cool, store them in the fridge. Use them to negotiate that fanny-patting privilege.

Wake Me Up Before You Go Go Caffeinated Brownies

Soundtrack: *Wake Me Up Before You Go-Go* by Wham!

Box of brownie mix	Bar of GOOD chocolate	Chocolate powder
Eggs	Water	Butter
Cinnamon		
Optional: 200 mg. tablets of caffeine from the pharmacy		
Optional: Cayenne pepper		

Boxed brownies are good. But, like breast implants, you can tell they are fake upon closer examination. They just don't have the right "mouthfeel," as they say in the business. Yes, we are still talking about the brownies.

Go buy yourself a fancy brownie box mix. Get one that is extra chocolate, caramel, or has something else extra pleasing about it. Can't go wrong with Ghirardelli, for example. Make sure you have on hand both eggs and oil. While you're there, pick up a bar of GOOD chocolate. If there is any doubt in your mind as to size, buy two.[161] You will also need butter, but then, when doesn't one need butter? If you don't have bittersweet chocolate powder, get some of that as well.

Tip:
Saying "please" and "thank you" to her is like getting a happy ending is to you. Try it.

Bust out your white lab coat and your safety goggles, because here is where we turn this brownie into solid energy. If the brownie box says it makes nine brownies (for example), then take nine of the 200 mg. caffeine tablets, and grind them up either in a mortar and pestle, or in a small bowl with the handle of a butter knife. Don't let a woman catch you doing that.[162] Grind the caffeine tablets into a fine powder. No, it is not to be snorted. **No, really, don't do that.** Add the dry caffeine powder to dry brownie powder from the box and stir together *well*, because this really needs to be evenly mixed. Do NOT use more than 200 mg. per brownie or we are not liable[163] for your not sleeping for a month. We are also not liable for your health. Check with your own medical professionals before trying this; we keep ours busy enough.

Follow the brownie box directions, but use melted butter in place of the oil, and increase the amount of butter by 25%. Also, melt the butter first on low heat in a pan, to drive off some of the water. Add one tablespoon of cinnamon, and stir until combined.

---

[160] It's the cook's natural right.
[161] This applies to most things. Pairs are very popular here.
[162] Women have this irrational belief that tools are meant to stay pretty and clean. We know, we don't get it either.
[163] A fancy word for, "You didn't follow the instructions, so pttttthhh."

This part is optional. For the Real Men™ out there, add about a half-teaspoon of cayenne pepper. Do not add more burn, napalm boy, or you'll ruin the brownies. The cayenne pepper is the nipple, not the whole boob. Capiche?

Now, break up the bars of GOOD chocolate into bite-sized shards, and mix those into the batter. Select whatever baking pan size the box recommends, butter up the pan really heavy, and then dust it with the chocolate powder. Pour the batter in, and spread it out even. Bake as directed, but DO NOT over-bake!

Allow to cool, then chill the brownies, and serve with ice cream or chocolate sauce. Preferably both.

On those strange twilight zone occasions that there are leftovers, freeze them, and eat them frozen. We don't recommend these after 6 p.m., unless you are one hardcore caffeine junkie. In which case, we salute you!

Killer Chocolate Cake

Soundtrack: *Girls, Girls, Girls* by Motley Crue

Read this recipe all the way to the end BEFORE you try it. On the way home early from work, swing by the store and get the following:

Box of chocolate cake mix (Yeah, it's cheating. You've read this book this far; don't get all judgmental NOW), and all of the required ingredients on the box.
Box of **instant** chocolate pudding
2 bars of the good *baking* semi-sweet chocolate (not regular chocolate, BAKING chocolate)
Big tub of extra creamy Cool Whip™ (leave this out on the counter when you get home)
Jar of chocolate powder
9 by 12-inch glass baking dish

Something like 98% of all women will want sex after eating chocolate. Okay, that's not ACTUALLY true, but it's close. Occasionally - okay, daily - you need to find a way to slide some into the ladies. We mean chocolate, of course. What did you think we meant?

Dump the cake and instant pudding powders into a bowl, add the eggs and water per the instructions on the box, increase the oil on the instructions by about 25 percent (just put MORE in, but NOT double). Stir the cake batter goo together as little as possible, but just enough so there are no dry powdery bits in the mix.

> Massage her achy bits. No, for longer than that. Breasts are not generally achy.

Prepare your pan or baking dish by smearing butter all over a pan or baking dish (using a paper towel to do the smearing), toss in a few big pinches of chocolate powder, and bang the dish around so that the butter is all covered in chocolate powder. If you just banged the dish on your granite countertop, throw the dish pieces away, sweep the floor, get a new dish, and start over, Conan. Pour the cake batter into the dish, and shake or spin it a bit to even out the chocolate thickness at the edges. Use a CLEAN hammer to bust up one of the chocolate bars, and place shards into a bowl. Do NOT break the bowl or your counter with the hammer, Neanderthal. Sprinkle some chocolate powder over the broken chocolate bits and toss it around in the bowl to coat the pieces of chocolate with, well, more chocolate. Sprinkle the chocolate bits all over the top of the cake batter, and put it in the oven, following the instructions on the box for the temperature and time for the pan or baking dish you have selected to use.

While that is baking, melt the other bar of chocolate, and prepare the chocolate cream topping. Look back at the Peppermint Pat-Her-Fannies (page 81) recipe if you don't remember how. Once the chocolate is melted, slowly stir it into the Cool Whip. When you think the cake is done, take a toothpick and stick it in the middle of the cake.

If the toothpick comes out clean, the cake is done. If you don't have a toothpick, lightly touch the center of the cake, and if it springs back like a high school erection, you're *probably* done. We still recommend sticking a knife in there to make sure. Let the cake cool 20 minutes. Go watch a *South Park* episode, or if she is there, something SHE will like to watch. Yeah, give her the remote and let her pick. Remember, this is about having a romp in the panties. Pre-dinner entertainment she likes may lead to post-dinner entertainment that **you** like.

Once the cake is cool, spread the chocolate cream onto the cake, and serve to your female companion.

Have a great line and move ready, because she should be warmed up and good to go after a cube of this cake. If you're really good, like us, have a table set up with some of the other recipes in the book, and feed her dinner. Nice plates, glass, and silverware set up CORRECTLY, with the sequence from left to right being: fork, plate, butter knife (sharp edge facing INTO the plate), and spoon. Even if you're a college student using plastic dinnerware, do it right. Candles in the center of the table, dim the lights, and don't set the place on fire, caveman.

When you bring her the cake, towards the end of her piece, suavely feed it to her with your fingers.[164] For purposes of this discussion, "suavely" means "Imagine how James Bond would do it." We are not talking about the car chase and shootout scenes.

Assuming you don't jack it up, that should do it.

If your conversational skillz occasionally leave you with blue balls, limit your conversation to how beautiful she looks, and how HER day went, meathead. You'll get some. Trust us.

The Unfortunately Named....Trifle

Soundtrack: *Cars* by Gary Numan

A work party is coming up. Funny-Smelling-Lady (FSL) from the other end of the office is working her way towards your veal-fattening-pen/cubical with a food sign-up sheet. We know your pain, Padawan. Sign up for dessert, and when she says, "You can't just bring donuts again!" tell her you wouldn't think of it, and smile. Two days or three before the office torture event, swing by the store and grab the following items. Read this recipe through before starting shopping.

Small Cake, yellow or white	Big tub of good Cool Whip™
2 Boxes of vanilla pudding mix	Bag of frozen mangos or peaches
Milk	

Biggest disposable clear plastic food tub with lid you can find that will hold all the above

When you get home, leave the Cool Whip™ on the counter. This is crucial to your success. Get the cake out; unwrap, or unbox it. Get out the big cutting board and cube up the cake. If you scored a cake with frosting, cut the frosting off with your 8-incher (chef's knife, dude, and that is NOT 8 inches; you can lie to her, but we know better.[165] Cut the cake so you have pieces about mouthful-sized, because more is just wasteful.[166] Set the cake cubes out onto a cookie sheet where they won't be in the way. Follow the plan of attack on the box for the vanilla pudding, and set it chillin' in the fridge once it is made. Open the bags of frozen fruit, and spill them out on a big plate to start thawing.

Go play. We prefer first-person-shooter games.

---

[164] You better have washed them well, grease monkey.
[165] Truth is, she knows better too, but she's playing nice.
[166] Wasted on some, anyway.

After about two hours of mayhem, set the big food tub in the middle of all the stuff you prepared. The cooking is over; it's construction time. Start out with the cake cubes, and layer them on the bottom of the food tub. Spoon some pudding over the top of the cubes, and smooth it out. Don't be too prissy here, sunshine, it just all needs to go in the hole with some room for the next layers. Spread the whipped cream over the top of that. Set pieces of fruit down now in another layer. Next layer is cake again, then pudding. Now more Cool Whip and another level of fruit. Keep going till you get about a finger from the top of your tub. Cover whatever layer you just made with more whipped cream, and set the last piece of fruit in the center. Cover and refrigerate. Take a big spoon with you to serve.

So that was easy, a mere trifle of effort on your part. They liked it, and so did you. Now let's kick it up into big boy gear. Hit the store, maybe two, and grab the following:

Yellow cake mix	2 cartons of heavy whipping cream
Jug of best whole milk you can find	2 boxes of cook and serve vanilla pudding
Fresh mango, if ripe; frozen if not	

Bake the cake per the box, but add a little pat or two of butter (melted, of course) to the mix before baking. When done, turn the cake out and cube it up. Set it out to dry overnight; keep the dog off of it.

Next day, or much later that day: make the pudding, but use the whole milk and chill. Use a whisk or a kitchen mixer (if you've got one) to whip the hell out of the cream to make... wait for it... whipped cream. For the better looking dessert, use a tall clear glass container/bowl to build into. Now get to work making your layers, paying attention to how it looks around the edges through the glass. Chill when you are done. Serve cold, with a big spoon. Don't tell anyone how much whole milk and cream is in it. They might never forgive you.

Pour Some Sugar on My Banana

Soundtrack: *Pour Some Sugar on Me* **by Def Leppard**

Along with apple pie, and not understanding the nature of the Republic that we live in, a banana split is a very American thing. Easy as hell to make if you buy the ingredients pre-made and build it. Hit the store and obtain, through generally legal means, the following:

Bananas	GOOD vanilla ice cream[167]
Lime sorbet	Mango sorbet
Chocolate sauce	Caramel sauce
Vanilla sauce	Can of spray Whipped Cream
Shelled pistachios	Fresh raspberries

As in many situations in life, you want to use a firm banana. The banana needs to be ripe, so look for a tinge of green by the stem, and solid yellow at the business end.

Believe it or not, you've been doing it wrong all these years. No, not that – we mean you've been peeling bananas all wrong. Once you try it our way, you'll realize that you've been dumber than a monkey for a long time. Grasp the banana at the stem end (the natural handle), and then pinch the other end of the banana like you'd like to pinch a nipple. We don't advise you pinch a nipple, unless she's into

---

[167] Don't be a cheap bastard; get something at least 4 bucks a pint.

that, in which case we advise it a lot. If YOU'RE into that, well, keep it to yourself. Back to the banana now. Once you pinch the non-stem end of the banana, you'll see the banana skin split easily so you can peel it back. Congratulations, you've graduated to Chimp. Pro tip: make the banana part "Bananas Foster" for a whole 'nother level of over-the-top goodness.

Get a bowl out. Any bowl will do, but a banana split looks best in an oval-shaped dish.[168] Peel the banana open, and slice it along its length to make two long halves. Set those in the bowl with two inches between them. Set up a second bowl the same. You are ready for some scoopage.

Place a round scoop of sorbet between each slice of banana at each end, and place a big scoop of vanilla in the middle. Pour chocolate sauce on the vanilla ice-cream; pour caramel on the mango sorbet; and vanilla sauce on the lime sorbet. Spritz some canned whipped cream in your mouth (like we needed to tell you to do that). Now spray some whipped cream onto each of the ice-cream/sorbet scoops, sprinkle with your nuts,[169] and then place a few raspberries on top for that king-of-the-hill look.

Get out the spoons, and try not to eat so fast that you freeze your brain. You may need that later. Or not.

Creamy Nut Cups

Soundtrack: *Candy* by Tom Petty and the Heartbreakers

Eventually it is going to be that day of obligations and pitfalls. Red Alert Day. You know - Valentine's Day. It is not commonly known, but the Catholics actually screwed this day up. "Saint" Valentine was actually a demon. Luckily for you, dude, we've got your back. You can already make little peppermint candies and brownies. Let's get you going on a creamy peanut butter cup.

Peanut butter	Bag of powdered sugar
Cream cheese	Bag of good chocolate, milk or dark
Small paper cupcake holders	

Scoop several blobs of peanut butter into a medium-sized glass bowl, add about a quarter of a block of cream cheese, and mix them well together. Taste. Keep adding peanut butter or cream cheese until the mixture tastes good. Add some sugar, stir, and taste. Keep at it until you have a stiff and sweet mixture. After all, a stiff and sweet mixture is your overall goal anyway, right? Cover the bowl of creamy nut filling[170] and place in the fridge.

Set out a bunch of the paper cupcake holders. Unlike you dorm-jockeys, we like organization; so cover a cookie sheet in plastic food wrap, and then line your cups in orderly rows on the sheet pan.

Melt half of the chocolate. If you don't remember, the steps are back on page 81. Spoon a little melted chocolate into each muffin cup. Pull the bowl of creamy nut filling out of the fridge, open it up, and use the cookie scoop or a spoon to take out a consistent amount of the creamy nut filling. Scoop the filling out of the spoon, and roll it in your VERY clean hands so it is ball-shaped. Set the creamy nut ball in one of the paper cups on top of the chocolate base. Repeat. Spoon in more melted chocolate over the creamy nut balls. Add enough to cover the filling in each of the muffin cups. Allow the cups to cool, or serve and eat them warm by gently inserting them one at a time into her luscious mouth.

---

[168] Don't ask us; we think it has to do with long things going well into oval things.
[169] Don't go there.
[170] Ewww. Even WE are not going to go there.

Get a pretty basket (red ribbons recommended). Take some of these cups, a few brownies, and some cookies, and you will have an "I made this for you with my hands of love" Valentine's Demon gift like no other. We know it's smarmy, but shut up and do it.

You know what to do next, right? Yeah, listen to her, and tell her she looks pretty, because she does. Remember, your yapping is probably the only thing that can bring those panties up faster than a cheetah on meth. When in doubt, act like you're the strong and silent type, even if you're the geeky and blathering type. Your Johnson will appreciate it.

afterward

Soundtrack: For Those about to Rock We Salute You by AC/DC

If you made it this far, you are truly a kitchen stud. We do salute you. If you have learned anything from us, it is that you should play with your food. Don't be intimidated by cup size, by the amount in your package, or what you haven't got in your cupboard. Improvise, soldier. If a recipe calls for pork and all you have is beef, well then, there's the beef. If someone fails to add bacon or butter to a recipe, well, there are few things that can't be improved by a little bacon or butter, right?

Food you made yourself is simply better. Unless you're spending more than $50 a person when you're out to eat, you probably can outdo the chef.

By now you should have hooked up some serious tail, and, if you haven't yet, you will. Use the skills we've taught you and try some other recipes. We'll keep putting them up at www.manmeetsstove.com. We hope to see you there. Thanks for coming along for the ride.

thanks

Soundtrack: *Lovin Every Minute of It* by Loverboy

We want to extend a sincere thanks to our editors: Scot Mathis, Phil Gilchrist, and the Teutonic Goddess, Elke Rechberger. Any remaining mistakes are either deliberate, or the mistake is ours, not theirs, we can assure you. We didn't need lube, but it was close, sometimes.

We also want to thank our Kickstarter backers:
Martha Natiuk, Ben Gardner, Lori Henriques, David Masuda, Kelly Alves, Deanna Cruise, Shortene, Keith Hall, Rohan, Jen Kimura, Esther Ryan, Mila Choe, Masahiro Kubo, Jessie Robertson, Aubrey Shaughnessy, Marjorie Joan Mannos, Rolla Woellhof, Rose West, Brooke & Jon Wollam, Kara Sjoblom-Bay, Mike, Greg Buchanan, Maria C, Jae Michels, Nathan Grunzweig, Jacob Bartruff, Kathy Jo Lorenz, Betsy Sochor, Cindy Vance Thompson, Matthew Camillieri, Bob Pilzer, Terry Bork, George & Roberta Smith, Marc Benzakein, Mary Bragg, Juli-Ann Williams, and Gary Raines.

A huge thanks to Katie Wood, the designer of our cover; Mythangelo for the diaper monkey; and Max Bork for the genius that is "Man Broccoli."

Thanks to the vast number of our friends that directly, or indirectly, contributed to our sick sense of humor. We couldn't do it without you, you sick bastards.

where to find shit in this book

D

E

F

G